IN THE KITCHEN WITH Elinor Donahue

IN THE KITCHEN WITH Elinor Donahue

Favorite Memories and Recipes from a Life in Hollywood

Elinor Donahue

with Ken Beck and Jim Clark

CUMBERLAND HOUSE
Nashville, Tennessee

Published by Cumberland House Publishing, Inc., 431 Harding Industrial Drive, Nashville, Tennessee 37211-3160

Cover and and interior design by Harriette Bateman.

Cover photograph by Engstead.

Library of Congress Cataloging-in-Publication Data
In the Kitchen with Elinor Donahue : favorite memories and recipes from a life in
Hollywood / Elinor Donahue with Ken Beck and Jim Clark.
    p. cm.
  Includes index.
  ISBN 1-888952-92-X (pbk. : alk. paper)
   1. Cookery. 2. Donahue, Elinor, 1937–   —Anecdotes. I. Beck, Ken, 1951–   .
II. Clark, Jim, 1960–   . III. Title.
TX714.D62   1998
641.5—dc21   98–38072
                                                CIP

Printed in the United States of America

1 2 3 4 5 6 7 8—03 02 01 00 99 98

*I would like to dedicate this book to
the memories of my mother,
Doris Donahue,
and my late husband,
Harry S. Ackerman,
for their love and nurturing
over the years.*

*And to Lou
for his patience, supportive
confidence, and unconditional love
that made this book possible.*

Contents • Anecdotes

Our Heroine Leaves Tacoma to Find Her Fortune in Hollywood

Father Knows Best and So Does Andy Griffith

A Career Filled by Family and Friends

Making The Most of Life's Stages

A New Direction

Contents • Recipes

Appetizers

Beverages

Soups and Stews

Salads

Breads

Breakfast and Egg Dishes

Banana Pancakes 51

Chocolate Waffles 50

Orchard Oatmeal 154

Swedish Pancakes 103

Eggs

Basil Breakfast Strata 252

Vickie's Brunch Eggs 226

Main Dishes

BEEF

Arlene's Brisket 107

Brisket Bracker 107

Chicken Fried Steak 36

Cornish Pasty 121

Hamburger Ackerman 147

Harriet Nelson's Corn Tortilla Pie 42

Liver and Onions with Bacon 101

Mom's Meat Loaf Ramoo 214

Mom's Pot Roast 54

My Tacos 35

Nana's Meat Loaf 261

Peanut-Bacon Cheeseburger 95

Shepherds Pie 132

Simple Supper O'Brien 46

Speedy Stroganoff Loaf 235

Steak and Kidney Pie 116

Susan P.'s Roast Beef 70

Swedish Meatballs 148

Sweet and Sour Ribs 22

Tamale Pie 238

CASSEROLES

Blintz Casserole 205

Cheese Grits Casserole 219

Chili Rice Casserole 203

Easton's Tuna Casserole Surprise 100

LAMB

Butterflied Leg of Lamb 161

Ghivetch (Lamb Shanks) 182

ORIENTAL

Chicken Sate with Peanut Sauce 245

Chow Don 141

Easy Pork Fried Rice Ramey 144

ITALIAN DISHES

Al Molinaro's Family Pasta E Fagioli
(Macaroni and Bean Soup) 187

Bourbon Pasta 244

Chicken Pasta Garry Marshall 188

Fettuccine Alfredo 240

Marie's Pasta 233

Mrs. G.'s Eggplant Parmesan 239

Spinach Parmesan 24

Spokane Pizza 74

White Clam Sauce with Linguini 90

PORK

Easy Pork Chops 72

Glazed Ham Loaf 171

Holiday Ham 62

POULTRY

Baked Chicken Breasts with
   Sour Cream 39
Baked Turkey Legs 73
Cheesy Chicken Bake 248
Chicken Fricassee 217
Chicken for Two 37
Cornish Hen and Wild Rice Supreme 86
Dijon Honey Chicken 241
Duckling Victoria 178
Mexican Chicken with Orange Juice 257
Oven-Fried Chicken 102
Poulet à la Nivernais (Chicken Braised
   in Red Wine) 104
Thanksgiving Barbecued Turkey 167
Wild Pheasant 130

SANDWICHES

Corn Dogs 159
Easton's Open-Faced Sandwich
   Supreme 100
The Grandma Special (Grilled Peanut
   Butter and Jelly Sandwich) 232
Tuna Salad Sandwich 150
Welsh Rarebit 211

SEAFOOD

Altovise and Sammy's Shrimp
   Sassy 84
Barbecued Soft-Shell Crab 184
Camarones Al Mojo de Ajo
   (Garlic Shrimp) 46
Crab Cakes 93
Crusty Baked Salmon with
   Lemon-Shallot Beurre Blanc 231
Dr. Bombay's Shrimp Curry 164
Egg Noodles with Tuna (or Salmon) 191
Fish and Chips 78
Mediterranean Roughy 156
Potted Shrimp 162
Salmon en Papillote 26
Sautéed Abalone 128
Seviche Sabrina 60
Shad Roe 31
Shrimp Creole Alto and Sammy 84
Shrimp Curry 27
Shrimp Hawaii 85

VEAL

Veal Chops with Arugula and
   Balsamic Vinegar 234

Side Dishes and Vegetables

Baked Tomatoes 158
Broiled Stuffed Mushroom Caps 175
Candied Yams 168
Carrot Pudding 65
Carrot Ring 48
Cauliflower Brian 134
Confetti Vegetables 32
Country Zucchini 136
Creamed Peas and Ham 135
Creamed Spinach Ackerman 231
Eggplant Provençal 77
Hessy's Celery, Peas, and Mushroom
   Medley 142

Condiments

Sauces

Desserts

Acknowledgments

This has been a grand adventure. During the first few days of planning, the house looked like a whirlwind had hit it. Digging up old photographs from the garage; sitting on the kitchen floor late at night and pawing through scraps of recipes; sharpening pencils; and making piles and piles of notes—that was the plan in action.

I could never have accomplished this task without Ken Beck and Jim Clark, whose knowledge and expertise in this genre were invaluable. I likewise want to thank all of the staff at Cumberland House who have worked to bring this project together and produce the book that you now hold in your hands. I have special thanks to publisher Ron Pitkin for believing in the book and to Julie Pitkin for her fine editorial work.

There are so many people to thank—especially all of those whom you'll meet in these pages—for being so generous with their gifts of time, recipes, and photographs.

There's Jane Wyatt, whose great-grandmother's rice pudding recipe was delivered to my doorstep before the phone was cold. I didn't know the U.S. Mail could move that fast! And my children and their spouses, who responded so enthusiastically and gave me almost more than there was space to use. And my friend and neighbor Peggy Ramey, who, when I was in doubt, cheered me on with her confidence in me and positive attitude.

I have special thanks for Lou, my husband, who put up with odd meals of onion rings and hard sauce for Christmas pudding. He kept smiling through many nights of take-out food, when, after writing about food all day, I couldn't face the kitchen. He was there to console me when the "gremlins" stole the photos that I could have sworn were by my side just a moment earlier. And he was there to quietly and calmly see me through the hardest few weeks in the beginning. To you I give heartfelt and loving thanks.

To all of you who've picked up this book to see what it's all about, thank you for your interest.

Much love to you all!

WELL, HARE WE ARE—At sixteen months old at my first home on Twenty-First Street in Tacoma, Washington.

Introduction

While sitting on my mother's lap on a bus heading for tap class at Reitha Gehri's Dance Studio in Tacoma, Washington, I read my first word. It was on a sign over a coffee shop and it said "DONUTS." I was not quite two years old and my delight in food was born that day.

My birth name was Mary Eleanor Donahue, and I came to the household of Doris and Thomas Donahue relatively late in their lives (my mother was forty and my father was in his early forties). My mother, older sister, and brother were great moviegoers, so I was going to the theater at a very early age and I'm sure Mother's dream was that one day I would be on the screen.

From my first movie contract at Universal, life in Hollywood has been as adventurous as an amusement park—a merry-go-round of jobs and auditions, a roller-coaster of triumphs and disappointments.

The Donahue family home in Tacoma.

After Universal, my next major stop was MGM, where I spent my happiest childhood years, and then the new entertainment phenomenon, television, came on the horizon and I joined the ranks of those stepping into those new waters.

The high point of my TV career, or at least the first, was *Father Knows Best.* Six years of hard work and a lifetime of friendships were made before I went on to my short stay with *The Andy Griffith Show.* On I went through the years—acting in television and occasionally in film or on stage in such diverse shows as *The Odd Couple, Days of Our Lives,* the film *Pretty Woman,* the wacky TV show *Get a Life,* and *Dr. Quinn, Medicine Woman.*

There have been lots of laughs and not a few tears along the many paths of my career, but successful marriage and motherhood have given me the most pleasure. And cooking, baking, and collecting recipes from many sources has been an ongoing hobby for years.

This is a collection of my favorite recipes. I learned to cook from watching my mother, and, as she never used a recipe, I didn't either. When I finally realized there was, for me, a decided lack of control of the finished product, I then began collecting recipes.

You'll notice that this cookbook is organized as a chronology of my life—with photographs and special memories accompanying each recipe. This, of course, is different from the traditional cookbook organization with sections of similar recipes going from, say, Appetizers to Desserts.

To make it easier to find a particular type of dish, we have arranged the Table of Contents by food category. So, though all of the desserts, for example, aren't found together in the book, they are grouped together in the Table of Contents. And with the detailed recipe Index at the end of the book, it should be easy to quickly zero in on exactly the recipes you want.

I hope you'll find some ideas here that you'll want to try in your own kitchen—and that you'll have as much fun doing so as I've had compiling this collection of memories and recipes from my life so far.

IN THE KITCHEN WITH Elinor Donahue

Our Heroine Leaves Tacoma to Find Her Fortune in Hollywood

Me and my brother Gerald, whom I called "Dayod."

Just Call Me Little Sister

Our family was somewhat different than most in 1937 in that my brother Gerald and sister Gwen were twenty-one and eighteen-and-a-half years old when I was born.

Gerald was a talented musician and artist, and Gwen was a professional dancer. She also shared the artist gene with Gerald. Early on I began to call them "Dayod" and "Dede," and those names have stuck to this day.

Before dinner each evening they would keep me occupied by performing for me and teaching me songs. Our mother was a wonderful cook, but Dede was also a whiz in the kitchen, and the following is one of her favorites.

SWEET AND SOUR RIBS

To the artist formerly known as Princess,
This is a very simple recipe but delicious!

4	pounds spare ribs
	Salt
	Water
½	cup water
4	tablespoons ketchup
½	cup white vinegar
3	or 4 drops hot pepper sauce

In a large pot cook the spare ribs in enough salted water to cover for 30 minutes. Drain them and place in a baking pan. In a small bowl combine the remaining ingredients and pour over the ribs. Bake at 350° for about 1 hour. Baste several times. When done they should be a rich, mahogany color, sticky, and delicious.
Serves 6.

Sister Gwen entertains me in my highchair at age four months.

My sister Gwen ("Dede") in dance costume.

In brother Gerald's arms on June 6, 1937.

An Old Pro at Three

Before my third birthday I started singing on a Saturday morning kiddie broadcast on radio station KMO in downtown Tacoma. I stood on a chair and sang such current hits as "Don't Sit Under the Apple Tree," "In a Little Red Schoolhouse," and "You Are My Sunshine."

After the show my treat was to have lunch before the bus ride home. I nearly always chose the same luncheonette. We sat at the counter and I'd order my "usual"—mashed potatoes and gravy and creamed spinach. Yummm!

The front door to home is always a nice place to be.

SPINACH PARMESAN

This is a modern version and even better, to my mind. You can cut the recipe in half or double it for a crowd, and it holds covered in a warm oven very well.

4	**10-ounce packages frozen chopped spinach**
1	**cup grated Parmesan cheese (Reggiano, please)**
½	**cup chopped onion**
⅓	**cup whipping cream**
2	**tablespoons butter, melted**
½	**teaspoon salt**
½	**teaspoon pepper**
½	**teaspoon ground nutmeg**
	Extra Parmesan

Preheat the oven to 350°. Butter a pretty 8-inch square baking dish. Cook the spinach according to the package directions. Drain and squeeze out the excess moisture. In a medium bowl combine the spinach, cheese, onion, cream, butter, salt, pepper, and nutmeg. Transfer the mixture to the buttered baking dish (a glass dish will do nicely). Top with extra Parmesan to taste. Bake for 20 to 30 minutes until heated thoroughly.

This can also be made a bit ahead of time and kept covered until ready to bake. Very versatile.

Serves 4 to 6.

At age three here I am already pounding the sidewalks of Tacoma and performing weekly on the radio.

YOU GET A LINE AND I'LL GET A POLE—With my fishing pole slung over my shoulder, I proudly make my way home with my fish that I caught at a place I called Muriel's Lake—reminiscent of Opie at Myers Lake in Mayberry.

Meet Me at The Fishin' Hole

Living near Puget Sound, my father, with some friends, would compete in the annual Salmon Derby. While they never won, the families were the recipients of some very large salmon. To this day it is my favorite fish, and I like to broil it simply, but this recipe is outstanding.

SALMON EN PAPILLOTE

Specialité de la maison Isabelle Lewis

4   to 6 salmon "sandwiches" (⅓ to
       ½ pound portions)
     Lemon juice
2   tablespoons butter
     All-purpose flour
     Water
     Grated Cheddar cheese
     Dill
     Worcestershire sauce
     Tabasco sauce
     Paprika
     Salt and pepper
     Sherry or Madeira
1   6-ounce can tiny shrimp
     Mushrooms

*Muriel's Lake wasn't just for fishing.
Here I enjoy a refreshing dip while playing with
my toy sailboat.*

If you have a cooperative seafood dealer, ask him to slash the thick part of the fillet the long way, so you have a "salmon sandwich" ready for filling. (This takes more explaining to the average fish man than you'd think, so be patient.) If you can't have this done, partially freeze the salmon, so it's easy to slash it with a sharp knife without tearing the fish apart. Then divide the fish into sections about ⅓ to ½ pound per portion.

Rub the individual "sandwiches" with lemon juice and carefully place them opened on dampened parchment paper or very lightly greased lightweight brown paper (the paper should be doubled). Make a lightweight sauce, starting with a couple of tablespoons of butter into which you stir enough flour to thicken just a bit. Add a little water to make a roux about the thickness of light cream (I cheat a little on this to cut starch calories—let it run; it won't matter). Then add some grated Cheddar cheese to taste, lots of dill, some Worcestershire, Tabasco,

paprika, salt, pepper, and lemon juice to taste—and, perhaps, a touch of sherry or Madeira. (I never note quantities because everyone likes to season differently.) Rinse, drain, and add the tiny shrimp which have been rinsed and drained.

Spoon this sauce between halves of the salmon "sandwiches" (ignore the running of the sauce), top the "sandwiches" with sautéed slices of mushrooms, and seal the paper bundles, using rubber bands at the ends if necessary to hold them firmly. You can refrigerate these earlier in the day and then remove them from the refrigerator about 30 minutes before putting them in the oven. Be sure the papers are moist. Bake at 350° for 40 to 45 minutes. Add a little sprinkle of water during baking. This ensures a thorough steaming.
Serves 4 to 6.

Vaudeville Trouper

I started singing and dancing in vaudeville at the tender age of four-and-a-half, playing theaters on the Bert Levy Circuit in the Pacific Northwest—Yakima, Spokane, and Seattle. One day, while in Seattle, Mother decided we would splurge on dinner at the famed Olympic Hotel. I was now six (having returned from Hollywood and my first movie) and doing five shows a day at the Palomar Theatre, and we both deserved the break. I ordered shrimp curry and was definitely under-whelmed. However, as the years went by, I learned to appreciate the spicy-yet-delicious flavors of curries, and here is my favorite.

SHRIMP CURRY

4   tablespoons butter
3   green onions, chopped
1   clove garlic, minced
3   tablespoons all-purpose flour
2   tablespoons curry powder
½   teaspoon powdered ginger
1   cup chicken stock
1   cup light cream
2   tablespoons fresh lemon juice
1   pound cooked tiny shrimp
    Rice

Condiments:
    Sliced bananas
    Chopped chives
    Chutney
    Chopped peanuts
    Coconut
    Chopped eggs

Here I am in one of mama's masterpieces.

In a large saucepan melt the butter and sauté the onions and garlic until soft. Sprinkle with the flour, curry powder, and ginger. Gradually add the chicken stock and then the cream. Cook and stir until well blended and thickened. Add the lemon juice and the shrimp. Adjust the seasonings. Serve over rice with condiments.
Serves 4.

My "mood" pose.

All Aboard for Hollywood

On December 7, 1942, Mother and I boarded a train to Hollywood. I'd completed my first tour of duty on the Bert Levy Circuit, and so we left Tacoma and the Northwest to seek our fortune in California. I was told my father wanted Mother to have a vacation, but the real reasons were kept from my ears. There were no discussions. I believe my father did want Mother to have a vacation, but who did what to whom, and when, is a mystery to me.

The trip down the Coast was beautiful, and because of it my love of train travel continues to this day. We left Tacoma with no place to stay in Los Angeles. Our only insurance was a few phone numbers in case of an emergency. That emergency seemed to be the minute we got off the train, because I recall a couple of nights with some of my father's kinfolk. My only true remembrance is that they seemed disapproving of Mother, though they were outwardly hospitable. The high (or perhaps low) points of the stay were that I burned my leg badly on a wall heater, and I had to eat prune whip, which tastes good to adults, but not to kids. We left that situation as quickly as possible.

Even at this early age, memories of Washington State and its wonderful apples filled my little-girl imagination. This apple crisp is to dream about.

My father took this photograph of me across the street from our house in Tacoma.

APPLE CRISP

6   **large apples, peeled and sliced**
½   **cup orange juice**
      Bit of Cointreau, optional
½   **cup sugar**
½   **teaspoon ground cinnamon**
      Dash ground nutmeg
      All-purpose flour
¾   **cup firmly packed light brown sugar**
¼   **teaspoon salt**
6   **tablespoons butter or margarine**

Arrange the apples in a greased baking dish. Pour the orange juice over the apples. In a small bowl combine the sugar, cinnamon, and nutmeg, and then sprinkle over the apples. In a separate bowl combine the flour, brown sugar, salt, and butter to make a crumbly mixture. Spread over the apples. Bake at 350° for about 45 minutes until the apples are tender and the crust is lightly browned.

    Variation: For a nutty flavor, add ¼ cup rolled oats and an additional tablespoon of butter to the flour mixture.
Serves 6.

"Meet Me At Third and Fairfax"

In 1934, on property owned by the A.F. Gilmore family, Hollywood's famed Farmers Market, at Third Avenue and Fairfax was born.

Such was its fame that almost as soon as Mother and I arrived in town we were directed there. Whether we purchased anything or not, the colorful stalls, piled high with fruits, vegetables, meats, and exotic items were a feast for the eyes and nose.

The best doughnuts and coffee were there, as well as a fish stall, where one could sometimes purchase freshly cracked Dungeness crab from the Pacific Northwest, easing our homesickness.

Today, of course, some things have changed. No longer can you see sausages being made, nor visit a stall that featured teas and pots from the world over, as well as very-special-occasion jams and jellies, and fat jars of pickled peaches.

But they still have the peanut butter-making machine and homemade ice cream and fancy cake decorating done in a window for all too see.

And they still have a Tusquella—Bob, to be exact. His father started Tusquellas Meats in 1942, and Bob began working for his dad in 1953. In 1966, Bob took over the seafood stall and has made it into one of the most successful operations there. His wife, Kathy, is in the act—supplying specialty items for the cases (fish salads, chowders, and even breads and cakes). And on occasion daughter Melanie helps out behind the counter.

I picked up some shad roe the other day, and it was sensational! But you've got to be quick. Shad roe season is but a scant ten-day to two-week period in April or May. The shad is a river fish found in the Sacramento and New York areas (Bob prefers the New York variety). Though the fish itself is not well thought of, the roe is prime.

I have to confess that I consumed the entire shad roe for two—alone, by myself!—the other evening. I hope you enjoy this as much as I obviously did.

You've got to hand it to Bob (seen here in his shop about ten years ago)—nobody crabs about the delicious seafood at Tusquellas in the Farmers Market.

SHAD ROE

1   large pair shad roe
1   to 2 tablespoons butter
2   cloves garlic, minced
1   fresh lemon, cut in half and seeded, if
      possible
    Garlic salt and pepper to taste

In a skillet melt the butter and sauté the roe over low heat (any higher and it will pop like popcorn!) for 5 to 6 minutes total, carefully turning once. Season on the top side after turning just that one time. When done, carefully transfer the roe to a serving plate and keep warm.

In the remaining butter in the pan sauté the garlic until just lightly golden (do not burn!). Squeeze the juice from half of the seeded lemon into the pan. Cook down for 1 minute. Season with garlic salt and pepper to taste. Pour the sauce over the shad roe, and serve immediately with the remaining lemon cut into wedges.
Serves 2 (or 1!).

P.S. Bob Tusquella now runs Bob's Coffee & Donuts in the Market, and in 1991, Los Angeles Magazine *voted it a Best in L.A. Award. Keep up the good work, Bob. Today the Market, tomorrow the world!*

A New Home in an L.A. "High Rise"

We found a second-floor apartment with kitchen privileges on Virgil Avenue in Los Angeles. Fine old craftsman-style architecture prevailed, and, as the neighborhood had fallen on hard times, the owners took in boarders. Mother and I were cozy and content there, even though Santa Claus was "unable to find us that year because we had moved." But I was happy.

One night we went to see a radio show. Admission was free and it was fine entertainment. As it happened, we chose to go to *The Spike Jones Show* on Vine Street above Hollywood Boulevard, and Jones and his gang of madcap musicians were as wild and spectacular a group of performers as you could ever find.

Spike's show was a clean, fresh melange of joy and silliness, and this vegetable confetti reminds me of him. This is great hot or at room temperature. It can "travel" and be reheated, so it's perfect for family gatherings, but it is also fine cold the next day. It's sort of quiche without crust.

Mother and I pose in front of the Beachcomber.

CONFETTI VEGETABLES

1   cup mashed, cooked carrots
1   cup frozen chopped broccoli, thawed
1   10-ounce package frozen whole kernel
    corn, thawed
1   cup milk
1   cup cracker crumbs
½   cup shredded sharp Cheddar cheese
¼   cup minced onion (fresh, not dried)
⅓   cup melted butter
    Salt
    Black pepper to taste
⅛   tablespoon cayenne pepper
4   eggs

In a large mixing bowl combine the carrots, broccoli, corn, milk, cracker crumbs, cheese, onion, and butter. Season with the salt, pepper, and cayenne. Beat the eggs until frothy. Blend into the carrot mixture lightly. Pour into a buttered, round glass baking dish, approximately 2-quart capacity (10 inches round and 2 inches deeep). Bake at 350° for 40 to 45 minutes or until a knife inserted near the center comes out clean. Serve hot or at room temperature, and it reheats (covered) very well.
Serves 6 to 8.

Spike Jones and His City Slickers during the 1940s.

Old Aquaintance Not to Be Forgotten

The announcer and warm-up man at Spike Jones' radio show was a handsome, middle-aged character actor named Richard Lane, who later became a TV sports announcer. He had been under contract to Universal Pictures for many years, and fans knew him, among other roles, as Captain Farraday in the "Boston Blackie" movies with Chester Morris. Later, he was featured in the Frank Sinatra-Gene Kelly musical *Take Me Out to the Ball Game.*

Mother gasped and grabbed my arm when Mr. Lane walked out on stage. "I know him," she whispered to me. "When your sister danced in Texas Guinan's Troupe, he was her straight man."

After the radio show was over, we went to the stage door with all the other fans, and Mr. Lane immediately recognized my mother in the crowd. He indicated for us to wait for him to finish signing autographs, whereupon he drove us home, asking Mother to tell him what all had been happening with us.

To make a long story shorter, he and his family took us under their wings. He was the only father figure in my life, and I needed one so much. He and his wife let me call him "Daddy Dick." He very shortly was responsible for my being cast in my first movie, *Mr. Big.*

The Lanes' housekeeper was a superb cook and baker. Her peach pie would make angels sing. In her memory, I present this for your enjoyment.

Daddy Dick and I split grins.

PEACH SUGAR CRUST PIE

Pastry for one double-crust 9-inch pie
Fresh peaches
1 **tablespoon lemon juice**
½ **cup firmly packed brown sugar**
2 **tablespoons cornstarch**
⅛ **teaspoon ground cinnamon**
⅛ **teaspoon ground ginger**
1 **tablespoon butter, melted**
Sugar

Prepare the pastry, cover, and set aside. Peel, halve, and remove the pits from the peaches. Crush 1 peach and combine with the lemon juice, brown sugar, cornstarch, cinnamon, and ginger. Quarter the remaining fruit and add to the mixture. Turn into a pie pan. Top with the crust—fluting and sealing to the edge of the pan. Cut slits in the top of the pie to allow the steam to escape. Brush the top of the crust with melted butter. Bake at 400° for about 40 to 45 minutes until the crust is crisp and golden brown. Serve with ice cream, if wished. ("If wished!" Daddy Dick would say, "If you're going to have ice cream, really have it! Lots!")
Serves 6 to 8.

My First Big Film

Mr. Big was a big thrill for me to be in because I had a major crush on its star Donald O'Connor. But at the same time, I took the preparations casually, as though this was a perfectly normal and natural thing I was doing.

The only time I broke down was when Donald bounced onto the set and said his line, "Hi, Muggsy!" Seeing him in the flesh was just too much for my little six-year-old self. So I cried.

One funny thing about that movie was that my nickname back home in Tacoma was Muggsy, and no one in California knew it. Talk about coincidences.

The movie also starred Gloria Jean and Peggy Ryan. Gloria Jean had always been a favorite of mine ever since seeing her in *If I Had My Way* with Bing Crosby. She was so sweet to me and made me feel comfortable on the set.

We still see each other occasionally, and her joy with life is just as apparent now as it was then. Here is a recipe she'd like to share with you.

MY TACOS

I was introduced to tacos when I was very young and "very hungry" and I always thought they were everything great all wrapped into one.—Gloria Jean

2   pounds ground beef
2   cloves garlic, crushed
1   1.25-ounce package taco seasoning
     Dash Tabasco sauce
     Salt and pepper to taste
2   bunches green onions
1   bunch cilantro leaves
1   head shredded iceberg lettuce
     Cherry tomatoes, sliced thin
     Shredded Cheddar and jack cheese
2   small cans black sliced olives
2   small cans diced green chilies
     Corn or flour tortillas
     Oil
     Taco sauce

In a large skillet brown the 2 pounds of ground beef until crumbly. Drain the fat. Add the crushed garlic, taco seasoning, and a dash of Tabasco sauce. Add salt and pepper to taste and simmer slowly, stirring occasionally.

Fry the corn or flour tortillas until crisp in any type of oil. Fill with the meat and remaining ingredients and add taco sauce, any kind. Save the leftovers. It's better the next day.

Serves 4 to 6 (or fewer, if the few are really hungry!).

Mary Eleanor Donahue at age 6 in Mr. Big.

My friend Gloria Jean.

A lobby card promoting Donald O'Connor and Peggy Ryan in their 1944 release, Chip Off the Old Block.

Pegged For Success

Peggy Ryan was a young girl of many talents—singer, dancer, comic—who continues to entertain and teach in her hometown of Las Vegas, Nevada. She and Donald O'Connor made many movies together and were a great team.

When I spoke with her recently, Peggy confided, "Donald had strange tastes in food. When we'd go to the commissary for lunch, he'd put saltines on his ice cream!" His favorite dish, she said, was chicken fried steak with cream gravy. Let's have a double order of that!

CHICKEN FRIED STEAK

2 pounds lean round steak
1 cup all-purpose flour
2 teaspoons salt
1 to 2 teaspoons pepper
1 egg, beaten
1 cup milk
1½ cups vegetable oil

Cream Gravy:
4 tablespoons drippings from skillet
3 tablespoons all-purpose flour
2 cups milk
1 teaspoon salt
½ teaspoon pepper

Tenderize the steak and cut in to steak-sized pieces. Mix the flour, salt, and pepper and place on a plate. In a small, shallow bowl mix the egg and milk. Dredge the meat in the flour, dip in the egg mixture, and then dredge in the flour mixture and again in the flour mixture. In a large iron skillet heat the oil until very hot, but not smoking. Place the steaks in the skillet and cook until golden brown—about 5 minutes per side. Drain on paper towels and serve hot with cream gravy.

In the same skillet combine the drippings and the flour, stirring constantly. When bubbly, add the milk, salt, and pepper. Stir until thickened. If necessary, thin with more milk.
Serves 8.

Peggy Ryan in the 1940s...

..and still tops in the 1990s.

And here's a favorite recipe of her own that Peggy shares with us:

CHICKEN FOR TWO

It helps to hum "Tea for Two" while cooking—it takes about three choruses.

2   **chicken breasts**
     Butter
     Light olive oil
     Mushrooms

Pound away on the chicken until it's thin. In a skillet heat the butter and olive oil over medium heat and sauté the chicken until done. A few mushrooms thrown in wouldn't hurt. For a big finish, serve with wild rice and a green veggie. *Serves 2.*

Peggy Ryan and Gloria Jean in a comic number from Mr. Big.

The Big Night

How about this dress and matching bow in my hair?

The first public screening of *Mr. Big* was a sneak preview at the Pantages Theater on Hollywood Boulevard near Vine Street. Mother and I took the trolley to the theater that night. When I'd heard that afternoon that we were going I became very frightened. I kept saying to Mother that "I couldn't remember it." I couldn't eat supper, and by the time she had me dressed and we were walking to the corner, I was fighting back tears.

"What is the matter with you!" Mother said.

"I don't remember it!" I said, as I began to cry in earnest.

"Remember what, dear?"

"My dance, I can't remember it."

Sweetly, she hugged me. "You don't have to remember. It's a movie. You already did it months ago."

She was chuckling to herself as I related that I thought the actors were behind the screen, and that it, like a magnifying glass, made them big so the audience could see. Somehow, when doing vaudeville and watching the movie between shows from the wings, I'd gotten it into my head that some of the people there were being shown on the screen. After all, I was just a baby.

I didn't really believe I didn't have to perform until we were shown our seats in the special reserve section and the lights dimmed. Seeing myself on film, however, was almost as bad as having to do it all over again. Frankly, after all these years, it's never gotten any better.

Near the Pantages Theater was a restaurant called The Pig 'n' Whistle. They had good home-made-style food. One of our favorites was their chicken croquettes, little pyramid-shaped fried chicken-like things resting in a vibrant yellow, thick gravy. Mashed potatoes, fresh peas, and a little paper cup of cranberry sauce completed the dish.

I could never recreate that recipe for you, but here is a simple chicken dish that I like, too.

BAKED CHICKEN BREASTS WITH SOUR CREAM

12   small white onions, peeled
2   large whole chicken breasts, boned,
       skinned, cut in half
1   teaspoon salt
¼   teaspoon pepper
       Paprika
2   tablespoons butter or margarine
½   teaspoon dried tarragon leaves
¾   cup sour cream

About 1 hour and 30 minutes before serving: In a large pot cook the onions in 1-inch of boiling salted water for 15 to 20 minutes or until tender, then drain.

Preheat the oven to 325°.

Sprinkle the chicken with 1 teaspoon salt, pepper, and paprika. In a skillet melt the butter and sauté the chicken until it is golden on both sides.

Arrange the chicken breasts in a 6 x 10 x 2-inch baking dish, and sprinkle with tarragon. Pour in any skillet juices, and then place the onions here and there in the dish. Cover the chicken breasts generously with sour cream. Bake about 50 to 60 minutes or until tender, and then serve.

Serves 4.

Have Song, Will Sing

In 1944 a movie called *Bowery to Broadway* was made, and what a cast it had. Maria Montez, Jack Oakie, Frank McHugh, Turhan Bey, and Rosemary DeCamp were all principals, but it was also the first major role for the multi-talented Ann Blyth.

I was to play Ann's character as a child, the daughter of a dancing duo from vaudeville (McHugh and DeCamp), who, to their dismay, can't dance a lick no matter how hard they try to teach her.

But when Ann Blyth comes on the screen you can see her talent is singing. And what a talent it is. She has had a long and varied career, and, as the wife of Dr. James McNulty, she has been equally successful in her personal life. Here's one of her favorite taste-bud tempters.

Ann Blyth.

ANN BLYTH'S SOUTHWESTERN CHOWDER

1   tablespoon oil
1   small onion, chopped
1   teaspoon garlic powder
1   1.25-ounce-package taco seasoning
      mix
1   egg, beaten
½   cup bread crumbs
½   cup cooked rice
1   14½-ounce can clear chicken broth
      (Swanson's)
1   15-ounce can frijoles negros (black
      beans)
3   tomatoes, diced
1   5.5-ounce can V-8 juice
1   tablespoon lemon juice
½   pound cooked, diced chicken

In a skillet heat the oil and sauté the onion until tender but not brown. Add the garlic powder and taco seasoning to the sautéed onion, and cook for 10 minutes.

Add the egg, bread crumbs, and cooked rice. Mix thoroughly. Add the chicken broth. Bring to a boil, and then reduce the heat.

Rinse, drain, and add the frijoles negros. Add the tomatoes, V-8 juice, and lemon juice to the soup mixture. Simmer to heat through.

If serving later, leave out the lemon juice. About 15 minutes before serving, add the diced chicken and bring to a boil and heat through, then add the lemon juice. Simmer for 15 minutes.

Unused soup may be frozen and used again.
Serves 6.

Ann Blyth in Bowery to Broadway.

Please Don't Hit The Baby

Honeymoon Lodge, starring Rod Cameron and Harriet Hilliard (wife of Ozzie Nelson of Ozzie & Harriet fame on radio and television), was the next motion picture that Universal Studios put me in. The part was teeny-tiny, and the most memorable thing about it was what I perceived to be a threat to my life and limbs.

After setting up the master shot, the director gives the work to the cinematographer and lighting director, and at that point the stars' stand-ins enter the set and make the moves already decided on.

They had no stand-in for me, as my part was so small. It consisted of sitting on a toddler-sized chair and watching an electric train go around a Christmas tree and looking happy.

The stars had left the set and before the stand-ins entered, it was decided I should sit exactly where I was. The lights were dim. All of a sudden I heard a booming voice from the catwalks about shout, "Hit the baby!" I flinched as the lights came on, and, after the shock of the moment passed, it was explained to me that "the baby" was a size of light, and to "hit it" meant to turn it on. You learn something new every day.

Harriet Hilliard Nelson was a warm and loving woman, and I met her several times throughout my life. I even had the pleasure of ice skating around the rink with her at the Polar Palace in Hollywood when I was ten or eleven.

According to son David Nelson and his wife, Yvonne, this dish was made each Sunday at her beach house. I know you'll enjoy it too.

Here I am loaded down with dolls in 1943's Honeymoon Lodge. *The rest of the cast includes Rod Cameron (in Santa Claus costume) as a wealthy young rancher playing St. Nick, Fay Helm (left), Martin Ashe (operating the electric train), June Vincent (second from left), and Blaney Lewis.*

HARRIET NELSON'S CORN TORTILLA PIE

¾ pound ground round steak
¾ pound ground chuck steak
1 large onion, chopped coarsely
1 20-ounce can tomato sauce
   Chili powder
   Salt and pepper
1 20-ounce can corn niblets
   Corn tortillas
   Grated longhorn cheese
1 can sliced black olives, drained

In a large skillet sauté the beef and onion. Add the tomato sauce, chili powder, salt, pepper, and corn. Line the casserole with a layer of tortillas, then meat sauce, and cheese. Top with olives. Repeat the layers. Bake at 350° for 30 minutes.
Serves 6.

One of TV's favorite '50s moms, Harriet Hilliard Nelson of The Adventures of Ozzie & Harriet, *which ran from 1953 to 1966. The show originated on radio in 1944.*

Christmas in July

Not knowing quite what to do with me, Universal dropped my contract in 1944, and my next job was at Paramount in *And Now Tomorrow,* starring Loretta Young and Susan Hayward. I played Miss Hayward's character as a child, and I was thrilled to do so as she was a favorite actress of mine and was so beautiful.

The scene I was in took place at a factory Christmas party where, as the owners' children, we—"Little Miss Young" and "Little Miss Hayward"—tossed candy to the multitudes. As it nearly always happens in the movie business, it was shot in July or August, and we were dressed in beautiful little fur-collared coats and hats and woolen leggings. Talk about using your imagination!

Since this makes one think about candy and Christmas, I'd like to share my mother's cooked fudge recipe with you. She seldom used a recipe and the fact that there are actual measurements to this is a miracle, but I've written it down as I found it in her journal. It is the best.

P.S. Here's a handwritten note I found from around this time.

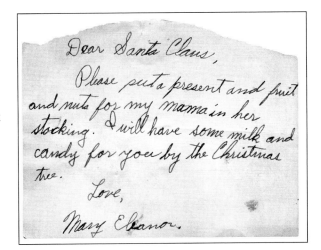

Dear Santa Claus,
Please put a present and fruit and nuts for my mama in her stocking. I will have some milk and candy for you by the Christmas tree.
Love,
Mary Eleanor.

MAMA'S FUDGE

1   cup milk
2   cups sugar
½   cup cocoa
1   tablespoon butter
1   teaspoon vanilla extract
    Nuts

In a saucepan combine ½ cup of the milk, the sugar, and cocoa, and bring to a rolling boil. Add the remaining milk. Cook to the soft ball stage. Remove from the heat and add the butter and vanilla. Cool to warm. Beat until ready. Add the nuts. Spread in a buttered 8-inch glass dish, and cool. Cut into squares.
Makes about 1 pound.

My mother and I dine with a set designer named Val, who took us to dinner from time to time.

O.K., now I have to confess that I have added a few more instructions to this myself because her original recipe, which she wrote down for me (she never measured anything—with spectacular results from time to time) actually read:

"2 cups sugar
½ cup cocoa
1 cup milk (½ first, ½ after rolling boil)
1 tablespoon butter
1 teaspoon vanilla extract

Cool to warm. Beat 'til ready. Nuts."

I kid you not!

Passages

Most of 1945 and '46 were slow years for me work-wise. Things were rough for us, as my father had asked my mother for a divorce after a short and unhappy trial at reconciliation. My grandfather (Pap-pap), who, along with my grandmother (Nan-nan), had lived with us for a short time, passed away, and Nan-nan returned to the Pacific Northwest where she became ill and died.

Mother, who had been a wife and mom since girlhood, was untrained in office skills and was unsure of herself and frightened, so she took a job at a nearby ice cream parlor. She made the best chocolate sodas I've ever tasted. Young men and women in retro ice cream and sandwich shops, take note. Here is her secret.

Me with my Daddy. Is sulking an inherited trait?

ICE CREAM SODA

In a soda glass put a liberal amount of chocolate syrup. Add a good scoop of ice cream and one squirt of soda water or seltzer. Stir well together. The glass should be about one-third full at this point. Add 1 or 2 more scoops of ice cream. Slowly add the seltzer, giving it a light stir with a long thin spoon or a straw as you go. Continue until you have a nice high head on it. Whipped cream and a cherry are optional.
Serves 1 well.

The back upstairs apartment we lived in from 1943 to '44.

Meeting Margaret

Things picked up for us in 1946 when I was cast in an independent feature, *Winter Wonderland.* It was a good and large part, the best I'd had so far. It can still be seen occasionally in the wee morning hours on some local television stations.

But the best thing to happen was a call to MGM to try out for a role in *Unfinished Dance.* To this day all I can remember is a dance audition, ballet only. I don't recall reading any lines for anyone, but I was ultimately given the role of Josie, Margaret O'Brien's best friend.

I was in awe of her talent and nervous about meeting her. But while I was standing in line at the commissary one day at lunch, she came up and introduced herself. She was so natural and friendly that it was hard for me to believe that she was one of MGM's most popular stars. We hit it off immediately and remain good friends to this day.

One of Margaret's biggest childhood hits was the 1942 film *Journey for Margaret,* a three-hankie tearjerker about some British children left homeless by World War II. Guess who played the American who came along and adopted her? None other than Robert Young, who, of course, adopted me as his TV daughter in the mid-1950s.

Margaret's heritage includes Hispanic, and I know she likes to eat shrimp, so for her I give you:

With Lynn Roberts in Winter Wonderland.

CAMARONES AL MOJO DE AJO (GARLIC SHRIMP)

1   pound medium shrimp
3   cloves garlic
½   teaspoon salt
1   teaspoon vinegar
2   tablespoons oil

Peel and clean the shrimp, leaving on the tails. Mash the garlic and salt to a paste. Stir in the vinegar. In a skillet heat the oil, add the garlic mixture, and cook, stirring a few moments. Then add the shrimp, stirring for 5 minutes. Serve at once.
Serves 2 or 3.

And here's a recipe from Margaret herself:

SIMPLE SUPPER O'BRIEN

Steak
Tabasco sauce
Worcestershire sauce
Ketchup
Sweet potato
Honey
Brown sugar

Marinate the steak in Tabasco, Worcestershire sauce, and ketchup combo. Serve with a baked sweet potato marinated in honey and brown sugar.

Margaret and I are playing our favorite game of jacks at the MGM studios around 1946.

Good Manners Pay Off

Before I actually began work on *Unfinished Dance*, my dance teacher, Thomas Sheehy, who was at that time president of the Dance Masters Association and who gave me my lessons free, sent us to Warner Bros. studio for an audition. They were looking for young toe dancers. I'd only been on pointe a couple of weeks, and I was pretty bad, but we went anyway.

After dancing I was dismissed with a bored "thank you." Before we left, Mother had an idea. She sent me back to thank them for seeing me and to tell them I'd only been "on toe" for a short while. This time they really looked at me, asked my name, checked me on the list, and, wonder of wonders, I got the job! Mother was no dummy.

Since we are now at Warner Bros. in this story, let's honor a famous bunny who came from their cartoon department.

Robert Young and Margaret O'Brien are seen here in 1942's Journey for Margaret. *They worked together again thirty years later in an episode of* Marcus Welby, M.D.

Margaret O'Brien (right) and I are together in a scene from Unfinished Dance. *The film took six months to shoot.*

CARROT RING

8   large carrots, sliced or enough to
      make 4 cups puree
1½ tablespoons butter
1½ tablespoons all-purpose flour
1½ cups milk
3   eggs, separated
½   teaspoon salt
    White pepper to taste
¼   teaspoon ground nutmeg
¼   cup sugar
½   cup slivered almonds
    Fresh parsley for garnish

Preheat the oven to 350°. In a large pot place the carrots in enough boiling salted water to cover, and cook for 15 minutes or until barely tender. Drain and purée the carrots in a blender or food processor or through a food mill. Set aside. In a saucepan melt the butter over medium heat and stir in the flour, cooking for 1 to 2 minutes. Gradually add the milk and stir until the sauce is thickened. Let cool for a minute and add the egg yolks one at a time, stirring thoroughly. Add the puréed carrots, salt, pepper, nutmeg, and sugar. Beat the egg whites until stiff peaks form, and gently fold into the carrot mixture. Then fold in the almonds. Pour into a buttered 8-inch ring mold and place in a pan of hot water, with the water reaching a height of 1 inch up the side of the mold. Bake for 45 minutes. Unmold on a warm serving platter.
Serves 6 to 8.

My dance teacher, Mr. Thomas Sheehy, gives me a pointer.

The dancer.

Scouted by MGM

One day during dance rehearsals the producer of *Unfinished Dance,* Joe Pasternak, brought a man to visit. He was a short, round gentleman who wore glasses and a natty three-piece suit. They stood off to the side watching intently. Mr. Pasternak pointed in my direction and whispered something to the man. They both smiled and watched a minute more and then they left. The man with the glasses was Louis B. Mayer, the head of Metro-Goldwyn-Mayer (MGM Studios), and I was shortly afterward offered a long-term contract. That began the happiest years of my young life.

There were twenty-eight little girls in the movie, the youngest was five and the oldest was eleven or twelve. Many mothers would bring special snacks to share, and I'll never forget one lady's chocolate waffles. They were cold, of course, and so we ate them like soft cookies.

Co-starring with Kay Burns (left) and Beverly McNeil (right), who were really good dancers, in the Warner Bros. musical short Melody of Youth.

That's the marvelous Cyd Charisse spreading her dress like the wings of a beautiful butterfly at center stage in MGM's Unfinished Dance. *I'm directly behind her right shoulder. I was nine when this publicity still was made.*

This shot shows the Merenblum Orchestra playing as we dance. Quite a dramatic backdrop, isn't it?

CHOCOLATE WAFFLES

2	eggs, lightly beaten
6	tablespoons sugar
¾	cup milk
½	teaspoon vanilla extract
½	cup chocolate syrup
4	tablespoons butter, melted
1½	cups cake flour, sifted
3	teaspoons baking powder
½	teaspoon salt

In a medium bowl combine the eggs, sugar, milk, and vanilla. Stir thoroughly. In a separate bowl blend the chocolate syrup with the butter. Let cool and stir into the egg mixture. In a large bowl combine the flour, baking powder, and salt. Add the egg and chocolate mixtures to the dry ingredients and stir until smooth. Bake in a waffle iron according to the manufacturer's directions.
Makes 4 or 5 waffles.

Breakfast at a Culver City Cafe

I could never eat breakfast—at least not when one is supposed to. So we would ride the two buses to Culver City, and by the time we got to MGM, an hour after we had left home, I was ready to eat.

There was a little cafe outside the East Gate of the studio where lots of crew people and actors congregated before work. I remember so well the steamy windows, the aroma of frying bacon, and the clank of coffee cups. And the pancakes. How I love pancakes!

Sharing a scene with Margaret O'Brien (left), MGM's most famous child star of the 1940s.

BANANA PANCAKES

These are wonderful. They cook up a very dark brown, so watch the temperature of your pan, so they don't burn.

2   **bananas, nice and ripe**
2   **eggs**
¼   **cup sugar**
    Pinch salt
1   **cup all-purpose flour**
1   **teaspoon baking powder**
½   **cup milk**
1   **tablespoon cooking oil**

In a large bowl mash the bananas. Add the eggs and mix well. Add the sugar and a pinch of salt. In a separate bowl sift the flour and baking powder together and add to the banana mixture, blending well. Add the milk slowly, blending in as you go. Last, mix in the cooking oil.

Wipe a non-stick skillet with a dab of oil, and heat the pan to medium. Pour a small amount of the batter in the pan and cook until the edges are dry. Then turn carefully to finish. Keep warm. Repeat until all of the batter is used. Serve with butter and syrup.
Serves 4.

Lunching at the MGM Commissary

MGM was a beautiful studio with a family feeling about it. The schoolhouse was a real old-fashioned two-room schoolhouse with a white fence around it. Mrs. MacDonald was the headmistress, and she ran a tight ship but lovingly. Some of my schoolhouse mates were Kathryn Beaumont (who later left for Disney where she was the model and voice for Alice in *Alice in Wonderland)*, Sharon McManus, Dean Stockwell, and Claude Jarman, Jr. In the high school room next door were Jane Powell, Elizabeth Taylor, and others.

The high point of everyone's day was lunch at the commissary. It seemed as though all the stars who were on pictures at that time ate there—often in costume, or nearly always in makeup.

And it seemed that people congregated in groups. Male stars like Robert Taylor and Clark Gable would dine at one long table, and the female stars like Greer Garson and Esther Williams ate at another. And the comics! They had their own spot behind the entrance to shield their sometimes overly noisy antics from bothering the others. The ringleader of that raucous group was Red Skelton, who often ended up standing on the table to tell a story. You knew things were about to go too far when you saw his red head poking up behind the barrier.

Salads are always popular at lunch, especially in California. This one is wonderful on warm summer nights too.

CALIFORNIA SALAD, NIÇOISE STYLE

I like to present the untossed salad to the "assembled" diners because it is very pretty and colorful. It's nicely filling and makes a satisfying meal with French bread and a light, lemony dessert.

Clean and crisp lettuce—red leaf, Boston, or your choice
Sliced hard-cooked egg
Pitted black olives
Crisp bacon, crumbled
Sliced fresh mushrooms
Peeled cherry tomatoes
Sliced cucumbers
Cold, cooked green beans
Garlic croutons
Rings of fresh red onion
Cold, cooked green peas
Roquefort cheese, crumbled
Cold, cooked new potatoes, sliced
A few anchovy fillets, cut in pieces

1 6½-ounce can tuna, drained and flaked
Vinaigrette (recipe follows) or Italian dressing

In a large bowl arrange the lettuce and top with any or all (heaven help us) of the remaining ingredients except the tuna, dressing, and Parmesan cheese. Place the tuna in the center. Toss with homemade vinaigrette or a good bottled Italian dressing and sprinkle with freshly grated Parmesan cheese.

VINAIGRETTE

¾   cup vegetable oil
¼   cup red wine vinegar
½   cup chopped onion
2   cloves of garlic, bruised
2   teaspoons Dijon mustard
2   teaspoons salt
½   teaspoon crumbled oregano
½   teaspoon crumbled basil

1   bay leaf, crushed
⅛   teaspoon freshly ground pepper

In a medium bowl mix all of the ingredients together and whisk to thicken.

Hold the Turkey Wing

As far as ordering food in the commissary, I had an average American child's appetite. I'd have rather had a hamburger or egg salad sandwich than anything fancy. They served good old-fashioned American fare, like roasts and chops, sandwiches and salads. One of the oddest meals I ever ordered was turkey wing fricassee. It sounded good. It smelled good. And it was what it was: A great huge wing on a plate. Squooshy and soft and covered with gravy, I took two bites and that was it. As the waiter told my mother, "I knew she wouldn't eat it."

Turkey wings are great, but let me share with you a pot roast that I like. There is nothing like the aroma of this cooking on a cold, rainy or snowy day, and the anticipation of eating it.

A growing girl's got to eat.

MOM'S POT ROAST

2½ to 3 pounds round bone or blade beef
    roast
    Oil or butter
    Salt and pepper
2   onions, sliced
1   or 2 cloves garlic, coarsely chopped
½   cup tomato juice
¼   cup beef bouillon
¼   cup full-bodied red wine
1   teaspoon crushed, dried basil
1   bay leaf
    Carrots
    Celery
    Potatoes

In a skillet brown the roast well on both sides in a small amount of oil. Salt and pepper and set aside on a plate to keep warm.

Add a bit of oil or butter to the pan. Sauté the onions and cloves of garlic until lightly brown. Put that aside with the meat and pour off all fat from the pan.

Return the meat and onions to the pan on low heat. In a medium bowl mix together the tomato juice, beef bouillon, wine, and basil. Pour over the meat and add 1 whole bay leaf. Bring to a light bubble. Transfer to the oven and bake at 275° or 300° for 3 hours or until "fall apart" done.

About 45 minutes before it is done, you can add the carrots (in large pieces), celery, and potatoes.

Serve with peas and crusty bread—a salad too—and you have a wonderful, easy meal.

Serves 4 to 6.

Rehearsing for Three Daring Daughters *are (left to right) Jane Powell, Jose Iturbi, me, Jeanette MacDonald, and Ann E. Todd.*

I Become Jeanette MacDonald's Daughter

While shooting *Unfinished Dance,* I was asked to test for a movie called *The Birds and the Bees.* It had originally been a play on Broadway and was now being brought to the screen as a vehicle for Jeanette MacDonald and José Iturbi, with Jane Powell as the eldest of three daughters. Eventually the title was changed to *Three Daring Daughters,* and it was a nice movie, perhaps most notable for "The Dickey-Bird Song," which made the *Hit Parade* chart for several weeks.

"The Dickey-Bird Song" is about the arrival of spring with a happy melody. This cake will make you feel as though spring has sprung.

MOCHA ANGEL FOOD CAKE

1   **cup butter**
1½ **cups sifted confectioners' sugar**
⅛   **teaspoon salt**
1   **teaspoon vanilla extract**
2   **egg yolks**
2   **squares melted bittersweet chocolate**
6   **tablespoons double strength coffee**
2   **egg whites, beaten**
1   **large angel food cake (one day old is easier to slice), sliced in 5 slices**
     Whipped cream
     Shaved chocolate

In a large bowl beat the butter until creamy. Gradually add the sifted sugar, salt, vanilla, and egg yolks. Beat thoroughly (by hand or mixer). Add the melted chocolate and then the coffee. Fold in the beaten egg whites. This takes a while because the mixture is slippery and difficult to work with.

Spread the mixture between layers and on top of the cake. Refrigerate immediately and let set for a day or at least several hours. Remove the cake from the refrigerator 1 hour before serving. Frost the cake (top and sides) with whipped cream. Top with shaved chocolate.
Serves 5.

From the pen of an MGM public relations whiz: What chance has director Fred M. Wilcox when three such charming young ladies as Mary Eleanor Donahue, Ann E. Todd and Jane Powell start turning on the charm—aided and abetted by José Iturbi. The quartet joins forces in Metro-Goldwyn-Mayer's charming Technicolor musical, The Birds and the Bees, *which features Jeanette MacDonald, Iturbi and Little Miss Powell. It was produced by Joe Pasternak.*

I watch from the piano stool as Jeanette MacDonald sings. Jeanette falls in love with and marries José Iturbi. The story revolves around the amusing complications which result when Jeanette attempts to keep her second marriage a secret from three young daughters who insist she is still in love with their divorced father.

A Frightful Scare

The test apparently went well, as I was cast and was having wardrobe fittings while still shooting *Unfinished Dance.* One day, while in our little canvas dressing room, we overheard a couple of mothers whose daughters were dancing in that film discussing that their little girls were being tested later that week for—*The Birds and the Bees!* Mother and I looked at each other in panic. She said, "Don't worry about it, I'll call your agent."

But I did worry. Here I was having gorgeous clothes made for me by designer Helen Rose, and others were still being tested?

For some reason whenever I'm anxious about something I crave Mexican food. "Hello? Dr. Freud?"

This was given to our family by some good friends in the 1960s, and it is super in its simplicity.

Dig the movie starlet in her cool shades.

THE BRACKERS' GUACAMOLE

2   very ripe avocados, mashed
½   medium onion, finely chopped
½   tomato, seeded and finely chopped
1   medium jalapeño pepper (from jar),
     with tiny seeds removed and then
     very finely chopped
    Garlic powder
    Salt and pepper to taste

In a medium serving bowl mix all of the ingredients together a short time before you're ready. Serve with homemade taco chips or any brand of commercially packed ones.
Makes 1 to 2 cups.

Jane Powell, Ann E. Todd, and I show off our finery for Three Daring Daughters.

Happy Dance

It turned out that prolonged casting calls were standard operating procedure at the studio in those days as a way to build up word of mouth about a particular film. That technique seemed to me like a pretty negative way to get the word out. However, I did the movie, and a grand experience it was. Ann E. Todd, a talented pianist, played the middle sister, and we were a happy cast—all five of us.

Mother was very content during this period of our lives because her cares had been lifted. And when she was happy, she liked to bake. Sunday was her only day to do so—and sometimes we were naughty. Occasionally she'd bake a butterscotch meringue or lemon meringue pie and that would be our dinner.

Here is the lemon pie, but eat a little something first.

LEMON MERINGUE PIE

Crust:

1⅓ cups sifted all-purpose flour
½ teaspoon salt
½ cup solid shortening
3 tablespoons ice water

Filling:

3 egg yolks
2 teaspoons grated lemon peel
⅓ cup lemon juice (2 to 3 lemons)
1 cup sugar
4 tablespoons cornstarch
¼ teaspoon salt
1½ cups boiling water
2 tablespoons butter

Meringue:

3 egg whites
¼ teaspoon cream of tartar
Dash salt
½ cup sugar

Working quickly, mix the flour and ¼ cup of the shortening to the texture of coarse meal. Add the remaining shortening until worked throughout (this should be very coarse). Add the ice water 1 tablespoon at a time, only until it comes together and you can form a nice ball. Let it rest in the refrigerator for a few minutes (you can rest, too).

Preheat the oven to 425°. Roll the dough out on a floured board (I use a pastry cloth with a cloth sleeve for the rolling pin). Place in a 9-inch pie pan and poke holes over the bottom and sides, after making a nice high edge. Bake for 10 to 15 minutes.

In a small bowl stir together the egg yolks, grated lemon peel, and juice. Set aside. In a saucepan mix the sugar, cornstarch, and salt. Gradually stir in the boiling water and cook, stirring constantly, for 2 to 3 minutes until clear and thickened. Carefully stir in the egg-lemon mixture. Cook, stirring constantly, for 2 minutes. Remove from the heat and stir in the butter. Cool for 5 minutes.

Pour the filling into the cooled, prepared pie shell.

In a large bowl combine the egg whites, cream of tartar, and salt, and beat until foamy. Gradually beat in the sugar until stiff. Spread over the pie in swoops and swirls. Be sure to seal the meringue to the crust to prevent "weeping" (its and yours). Bake in a 350° oven for 12 to 14 minutes, or until golden brown.
Serves 6 to 8.

GLEESOME THREESOME: Jane Powell (right) is backed by her screen sisters Ann E. Todd and Mary Eleanor Donahue in Three Daring Daughters.

WORDS A HOLLYWOOD PRESS AGENT MIGHT HAVE WRITTEN: First Impression—José Iturbi turns on the charm to impress his three "new daughters"—all of this before the trio discovers he has married their mother, Jeanette MacDonald. The scene is from Metro-Goldwyn-Mayer's melody-packed picture Three Daring Daughters, *co-starring Miss MacDonald, Iturbi, Jane Powell, Ann E. Todd, and Mary Eleanor Donahue. Filmed in Technicolor, it was directed by Fred M. Wilcox and produced by Joe Pasternak.*

Foreign Agent

We finished *Unfinished Dance* on a Saturday and started *Three Daring Daughters* on Monday. Mother said I was the only nine-year-old in town with bags under her eyes.

Mrs. Ray was our on-set teacher, and she was great. I loved her. The older girls in our three-student classroom were studying French and Spanish, so I got a dash of that, too, to go with my readin' and writin'.

GRIN AND BEAR IT—The baggy eyed girl, tired from working on back-to-back films.

SEVICHE SABRINA

This recipe has a definite South of the Border taste and is so easy to prepare. It is from a friend of a friend named Sabrina.

1 pound fresh fish sole (halibut fillets)
   Juice of 5 big lemons
2 tomatoes, peeled, seeded and finely
      chopped
   Half bunch cilantro
   Half bunch parsley
2 green onions or 1 small onion
5 to 6 dashes Tabasco sauce
¼ cup olive oil

In a glass bowl chunk the fish and cover with citrus juice. Place in the sun for two hours or on the sink for 5 hours. Add the other ingredients and refrigerate until cold. Serve with tortilla chips.
Serves 4 to 6.

Jane Powell, Ann E. Todd, and I kept up with our school work during the filming of Three Daring Daughters *thanks to our teacher, Mrs. Kay Ray.*

My First Pet

It seemed that Christmas that year would be spectacular. Working on a movie, making new friends, and receiving a regular weekly check was wonderful. I got a really terrific gift, but, unfortunately, it made one person very upset and angry.

Our first assistant director on *Three Daring Daughters* was called the Colonel. I never knew his real name. He took mother aside one day early in December and asked if I would like a kitten and would Mother allow it. She adored cats, and we had no pets, so she enthusiastically said yes.

On the last morning of filming before the Christmas break, he presented me with a tiny, gold-colored, mixed Persian male kitty. I was thrilled and enchanted as he was my first pet ever. I named him "Colonel" after you-know-who.

I ran onto the set holding him and shouting, "Look! Look what I got for Christmas!"

Everyone gathered around to see and compliment me—except for Miss MacDonald, whose face clouded over. She drew herself up and coldly walked past me, putting a bit of a damper on things, as you can imagine. Everyone around me murmured that we'd better get back to work.

I didn't find out until after Christmas what it was that had made her so upset. She had purchased a pure-bred Angora for me and was keeping it a secret, to give me at our Christmas party that afternoon, and I had spoiled her surprise.

My mother was distraught when she heard, but it wasn't our fault after all. However, to her dying day Mother never forgot it and wished we'd had that Angora cat.

But to a nine-and-a-half-year-old with a little

Tea time on the set as I bring a hot cup to Miss MacDonald.

kitten, nothing bothered me that day, and we had a grand Christmas banquet on the set.

Here is probably the best ham recipe I've ever made, and it is great for holiday buffets. It reads strangely but don't be dismayed. It works.

HOLIDAY HAM

1   20-pound ham
    Cloves
1   large jar Gulden's brown mustard
      (Dijon-style)
1   1-pound box dark brown sugar
1   large jar King Kelly Orange
      Marmalade
¼   cup vermouth

Score the ham and stud it with cloves. Cook the ham fully at 350° for 20 minutes per pound. Remove the ham from the oven 20 minutes before it is done. Completely cover the ham with the brown mustard. Next, spread the dark brown sugar over the ham and then spread on the marmalade.

Return the ham to the oven for 20 minutes to allow the sauces to combine. They form a big puddle around the ham, and this is the point when you might get discouraged. Please don't be.

Remove the ham from the oven. Pour the vermouth over the ham. Place the ham on a platter and keep warm in the oven (lower the heat to 200°). Pour the sauce from the baking pan into a saucepan and warm on the stove. After it's good and hot, place in a pretty sauce dish and pour over the ham as it is served.

As you can see, near the end there is a point at which it can be "put on hold" in case dinner is delayed. It is terrific.

You'd just about think Jeanette MacDonald really was my mom. Pretty good acting.

Great Spuds

I can't let the Holiday Ham get away without sharing this with you. These scalloped potatoes are so good with it. For a 20-pound ham you'd probably want to double it. However, for a quiet dinner the next day, this recipe will be fine.

SCALLOPED POTATOES

1   10¾-ounce can Cheddar cheese soup
½   cup milk
4   cups thinly sliced potatoes
1   small to medium onion, thinly sliced
    Butter
    Paprika

Mix together the soup and milk. Set aside. Butter a casserole dish and layer the potatoes, onion, and sauce in about three layers (depends on the type of pan you use—maybe two layers if it's a big square one). Dot the top with butter and sprinkle with paprika.Cover. Bake at 375° for 1 hour.

Remove the cover and bake for 15 minutes or until nicely brown and bubbling. Let it rest a moment before serving. It also reheats very well.
Serves 4 to 6.

Mutual Admiration Society: José Iturbi and Mary Eleanor Donahue defy the script writers and become pals during the filming of Three Daring Daughters *in which the characters carry on a cinematic feud.*

Christmas Turkey

That Christmas of 1946 was memorable in so many ways. Not only did I have a new kitten, but Mother went all out as Santa Claus because she'd not been able to for years. Santa brought a beautiful Mme. Alexander doll in a fancy pleated silk dress, lots of pretty new clothes for me, and a stocking filled with fruit, candy, and other small treats. Our hearts were filled with love and contentment and the anticipation of a good Christmas dinner.

As I've mentioned before, my mother never followed recipes, not really. I mean she might look at one and decide to try it, but she wouldn't look at it again unless something went wrong, when she'd say, "Oh, *that's* the way it's supposed to go!" By then, it was too late.

Sitting pretty.

In fact, I remember when pressure cookers first came out, Mother bought one and decided to stew a chicken. All was going well until she decided at some point that surely the chicken must be "done." But the lid wouldn't come off no matter how hard she tugged on it. Determined to get that lid off, she got a hammer. She banged and banged, and all of a sudden, the top flew up to the ceiling like a missile—with chicken broth going everywhere! The lid landed not a foot from where Mother was standing, transfixed by this horrible spectacle. It was then that she read the directions telling her to wait a length of time for the pressure to subside before opening the cooker.

A week or so after cleaning up the mess, we found a lone chicken wing draped over the curtain rod. By then, we could have a good laugh over it.

The moral of the story is: It's fine to fly by the seat of your pants when cooking, but if there's a recipe or recommended procedure, at least follow it the first time.

Anyway, Mother made the best turkey stuffing I've ever eaten, and the best turkey. Nothing she did would be popular today. She even stuffed the bird the night before. She said it made the flavors blend! So I won't share any of that with you, and you all have your own holiday traditions.

But I do want to give you her Christmas pudding recipe. I've never heard of one quite like it. The recipe is very old. It came from her mother and back through the mists of time, I guess.

It's called Carrot Pudding. Now I know that sounds terrible, but it really is fantastically delicious. Moist and sweet, also very rich, a little goes a long way, and it's quite easy if one has a food processor.

Mother ground all of the ingredients by hand. I have her old hand-grinder in my antique collection. Unbelievable. She made this recipe with that old grinder until she was well into her eighties. Well, God bless her, here it is.

CARROT PUDDING

1 cup ground carrots
1 cup ground potatoes
1 cup currants
1 cup suet (have butcher grind this for you)
1 cup sugar
1 cup raisins
1 teaspoon baking soda
1 teaspoon salt
  Grated lemon peel or ground nutmeg to taste

Hard Sauce:
3 cups confectioners' sugar
4 tablespoons softened butter
¼ cup (scant) hot water
½ teaspoon lemon juice
¼ teaspoon vanilla extract

In a large bowl combine the carrots, potatoes, currants, suet, sugar, raisins, soda, salt, and lemon peel. Blend together well and place the mixture in a buttered pudding mold (Mother used coffee cans with fabric tied over the tops). Place the mold in a larger pan of hot water and steam for 2 hours or so.

In a large bowl mix together the sugar, softened butter, lemon juice, and hot water until smooth and creamy. Beat in the vanilla and put on a buttered plate by rounded teaspoons. Refrigerate until needed. And watch out. People have been known to filch them for candy.

ART IMITATING LIFE—A scene from Father Knows Best *dealing with a kitchen mishap. As Mother would say, "Oh, that's how it's supposed to go!" Another recipe not followed.*

TO DIE FOR—Dreamy Peter Lawford on an MGM set in 1949.

In A Tizzy Over Peter Lawford

My tenth birthday was a big one for me. I'd been waiting for it for so long. To be ten! I was almost grown up. I had developed an enormous crush on Peter Lawford as had most of the female population in the world by 1947. Mother said she could always tell when he walked into the commissary by the silly grin I'd get on my face.

When asked what I wanted for my birthday, there were two things: a blue two-wheeler bike that I could see in a store from the window of the bus we took each morning to MGM, and to meet Peter Lawford.

A tall and warmly business-like woman in the publicity department, Anne Strauss, caught wind of the Lawford request and made the arrangements.

On my birthday she came over to our table at lunch to wish me a happy day and asked Mother if she could borrow me for a moment. Yes, she took me directly to Mr. Lawford. I nearly fainted. His face, that British-accented voice, those eyes. I was in a swoon.

He signed a picture to me and wished me well and I returned to our lunch table as if in a dream. I don't remember a thing more about that important day I'd waited so long for. But, I also got the bike.

Since I'm in a swoon mode, this salad is heavenly. Good with cold roast chicken or leftover ham, it can be made the day before serving.

HEAVENLY AMBROSIA SALAD

1   cup pineapple chunks, drained
1   cup mandarin oranges
1   cup mini-marshmallows
1   cup shredded coconut
1   cup sour cream

In a large bowl combine all of the ingredients. Cover and chill overnight.
Serves 6.

One more picture of Peter Lawford—for good measure!

An Ice Time with Margaret

Margaret O'Brien and I got to work together again in 1947 in a film called *10th Avenue Angel,* which also starred Angela Lansbury and George Murphy. It was a troubled production. Writers had been replaced, the script rewritten, and, as I recall, it had a change of directors at one point. They were writing it as they went, because a scene was added, in midstream so to speak, to introduce a friend for Margaret's character, and that's why I was cast.

The scene was relatively short but difficult timing-wise as it was a "walk and talk" shot. The camera, mounted on a crane and dolly track, followed us down a block to a corner where we were given shaved ice cones. Then we continued across a street. It was shot on the back lot of MGM, and, boy, was it hot. Thank heaven for the shaved ice cones.

Back on Unfinished Dance *with Margaret O'Brien.*

However, it took so long to set up and rehearse that the character actor, who had many fine credits to his name but was quite portly, began to suffer heat stroke. He was playing the ice cone man, and he couldn't remember his lines. We tried all morning. We broke for lunch. Margaret and I had our schooling. We tried to shoot it all afternoon but to no avail. We would have to return the next day and try again.

When we got on the set, after hair and makeup the next morning, who do you suppose was now playing the ice cone man? It was Daddy Dick (Dick Lane). What a treat to work with him, and he was right on. We got the shot in a couple of hours, and it was over by 11:30 or so.

By the way, Margaret and I got our choice of flavors for the cones. I think she chose mixed fruit, but I had root beer and must have consumed about one hundred of them in the two-day shoot. Needless to say, we didn't want lunch.

Seems like just a little snack would be good now. These are easy and delicious.

OYSTERETTE MUNCHIES

1   16-ounce box unsalted oysterettes
1   package ranch dressing mix
1   teaspoon dried dill weed
1   teaspoon lemon pepper seasoning
¼   teaspoon onion salt
½   teaspoon garlic salt
1   cup Wesson oil

In a shallow pan combine the oysterettes, dressing mix, dill weed, lemon pepper, onion salt, and garlic salt. Mix the above well; then heat the oil to just hot to the touch, but not boiling. Pour over the oysterettes mixture. As you pour the hot oil over the mixture, stir at all times. Then with a large spoon, keep turning until all of the oil is absorbed. Let cool thoroughly and put in a jar with a tight lid or any container that can be closed tightly. Keeps for weeks.

Suggestion: Put some in the largest plastic bag you can find and give it to friends. It will make their day.

Out of Work

I didn't do much for the rest of 1947, except learn how to do fractions at the schoolhouse and appear in a couple of shorts and do some work in the sound department dubbing lines for other children, mostly small boys. One voice I did was of the little brother of Annie Oakley in the musical, *Annie, Get Your Gun.*

In 1948, Metro-Goldwyn-Mayer changed forever. A big strike hit the whole industry, and by 1950 Louis B. Mayer was replaced as the head of the studio, and Dore Schary took over. Many contract people were let go, and I was among them. It had happened during the summer after school had let out, and Mother for some reason didn't tell me.

All summer I looked forward to returning to the schoolhouse and friends. We'd gotten me a sharp-looking plaid dress and a navy coat and shoes. The day before school was to begin Mother "fessed up."

I felt as though the bottom had dropped out of my life, and I became hysterical. If this had been Victorian times, you could say I had the "vapors." Cold cloths were applied, etc. However, the next day, with my face puffy from crying but with me proudly adorned in my new finery, we walked to the school that Mother had enrolled me in, Long's Professional School. It looked like the Bates Motel of schools. There before us stood a big brown clapboard house on a side street in the heart of Hollywood. It was, though, a pretty good school. There were some terrific teachers and some very nice students.

If you don't know about professional schools, they are set up to provide four consecutive hours of study each day so that afternoons are free for dance or music lessons and auditions for work. Hollywood Professional School was the prince among such institutions. Long's, I'm afraid, was the pauper.

Whenever a day seems gloomy, a nice pot of soup is a good thing to have. Here is one that I've made for years, on good days and bad, but I hope all of yours are good ones.

SPLIT PEA SOUP

1	pound split peas
2	quarts water
½	pound ham scraps, chopped or a leftover meaty ham bone
1	small onion, chopped
1	cup celery, chopped
1	carrot, sliced
1	6-ounce can tomato paste
2½	teaspoons seasoned salt
¼	teaspoon pepper
¼	teaspoon thyme
1	bay leaf
1	10¾-ounce can chicken broth

In a large Dutch oven or soup pot combine the peas, water, ham, onion, celery, carrot, tomato paste, salt, pepper, and thyme with the bay leaf. Bring to a boil. Cover, reduce the heat to simmer, and cook for 1 hour and 30 minutes to 2 hours or until the peas are tender. Stir occasionally.

Remove the bay leaf and ham bone, returning any meat to the pot and stir in the chicken broth. Heat thoroughly.
Serves 6 to 8.

Singing in the Kitchen

During my time at Long's School, I managed to squeeze out some work. The first job was a low-budget musical drama taken from a Louisa May Alcott book, *An Old-Fashioned Girl.* The star was Gloria Jean, who had also starred in *Mr. Big,* and Irene Ryan, who went on to fame and fortune as Granny in *The Beverly Hillbillies* TV series. The rest of the cast included beautiful Frances Rafferty, Jimmy Lydon, and others, who, like myself, were refugees from bigger and better movies.

And, boy, was I getting tall. To my mother's horror, I'd shot up that year over five inches. No more little girl parts for me.

One of the fun moments in the picture was singing the "Kitchen Serenade" number with Gloria and Frances, which brings me back to food.

This roast beef method was given me many years ago by my step-daughter Susan Peterson, who'd get it in the oven, leave with her husband and three children to visit friends, and then come home and eat dinner.

I'm growing up.

On the set of An Old-Fashioned Girl *are (left to right) Irene Ryan, Gloria Jean, Frances Rafferty, and me.*

Gloria Jean and Frances Rafferty have got my head in a pot as we sing "Kitchen Serenade" in An Old Fashioned Girl.

SUSAN P.'S ROAST BEEF

From the butcher get a prime rib roast of exactly 4 ribs.

Let the meat be at room temperature. Preheat the oven to 500°. Season as desired. In a shallow roasting pan, put the meat rib side down. Roast in the oven for 45 minutes. At the end of this time, turn off the oven. Do not open, do not peek, for 2 hours and 15 minutes. It will be a perfect medium rare.

I Was Doris Day's Daughter

In 1949 I performed in three movies: *The Singing Guns,* starring Vaughn Monroe and notable mostly for being a vehicle for his singing "Ghost Riders in the Sky"; *The Happy Years,* starring then-child star Dean Stockwell; and *Tea for Two,* a Warner Bros. musical starring Doris Day, Gordon MacRae, Gene Nelson, Billy De Wolfe, and Eve Arden.

Gene Nelson in the mid-1950s.

The Singing Guns was the first time I'd ever shot at night, and I thought that was very glamorous and exciting. At least for a little while, that is—until it got really cold and I got sleepier and sleepier. My part was a "silent bit" as I sat beside Vaughn Monroe in a horse wagon that was going hell-bent for leather with flaming buildings all around us as he sang "Ghost Riders in the Sky." I think. Maybe I was dreaming. So much for the glamour of "night shoots."

As for *Tea for Two,* Mother and I got the call to be at Warner's one afternoon and for me to be prepared to dance the Charleston, a popular dance of the roaring twenties. I didn't know any "Charleston." I was a ballet dancer, for heaven's sake!

As it happened there was a movie playing on Hollywood Boulevard, *The Fabulous '20s,* and it was all film clips and newsreel footage narrated to give the history of that era. I saw the Charleston danced. I went to Warner's and copied what I'd seen, and I got the part as Doris Day and Gordon MacRae's daughter.

Gene Nelson, who was also in the movie, was a multi-gifted fellow who, to my thinking, never reached the level of stardom that he deserved. He was a fantastic dancer and a charming actor, and possessed a sweet, normal-sounding singing voice that was very well suited to the roles that he played.

His most famous part was as the delightful Will Parker in the MGM musical *Oklahoma!,* in which he was, as always, superb. His wife, Miriam, also a wonderful dancer and singer, performed with him in many films. Gene later became a director of note in television and later still a teacher of his crafts at various universities.

Before his death, I had the pleasure of his friendship, and, though Gene and Miriam had divorced, they remained close, so that all who knew them could stay friends with both. I count Miriam as one of my dearest friends, and it is from her that I got this recipe.

Gene and then-wife Miriam and their son Chris are busy making a delicious concoction.

EASY PORK CHOPS

¾-inch-thick pork chops
Salt
Onions
Wine (white or red)

Cover the bottom of a frying pan with a thin layer of salt. Heat the pan, put in the pork chops, and brown on both sides. Cut up a yellow onion in chunks and sprinkle all over the top. Pour about a cup of red or white wine on the chops. Put on a lid, turn the heat down, and cook for 20 to 30 minutes.

DRESSED TO A TEA—Gordon MacRae (far left) and Doris Day (far right) headed the cast for Tea for Two, *which also featured S.Z. Sakall (in back) and Johnny McGovern, and me.*

Horsing Around

I forgot a film—*Arkansas Swing.* Maybe it should be forgotten since it is probably one of the worst movies ever made. To tell you how bad it was, it opened with much fanfare in the hometown of the stars, The Hoosier Hotshots, and it was pulled from the theater before the week was up, never to be seen again. The guys were charming and talented, but the movie was bad.

Making merriment with The Hoosier Hotshots in Arkansas Swing. *Watch out for the horse.*

And the filming certainly had its problems. One day during a take, a horse stepped on my foot, and on another day a horse head-butted the leading man and broke his nose. I had fun making the film though, because I loved playing a tomboy and being around the horses. Except for that, it was highly forgettable.

So in honor of that film, how about a turkey recipe.

BAKED TURKEY LEGS

2 small to medium whole turkey legs
1 packet dry onion soup mix (I use no salt because the soup mix has plenty)
½ cup (more or less) melted butter
Freshly ground pepper

In a roasting pan with a tight-fitting lid, brush the under side of the turkey legs with melted butter, and season with a bit of pepper. Turn over and brush the skin side with the butter and a sprinkle of pepper. Give the packet of dry soup mix a good shake and sprinkle the contents over and around the legs. Put on the lid of the roaster. Bake at 350° for 1 hour and 30 minutes.

Remove the lid and continue to cook, basting from time to time with the accumulated juices, for 1 hour and 30 minutes more or until tender and done.

School Daze

By 1950 Long's School moved to new quarters on a brighter, nicer street north of Hollywood Boulevard in a large and airy former private residence. The classes were full, mostly with seniors, and after they graduated there were just a handful of us left, and so the school began to fail. Wonderful teachers like Mr. Gruener and Mrs. Edwards were not retained because Mrs. Long couldn't afford to pay them. Near the end it was pretty much five kids and a room of books and we did the best we could. Poor Mrs. Long began to fail and some days she wouldn't even come downstairs to guide us through our self-planned studies. I was in the seventh grade.

When my sons were in the seventh grade, they just loved pizza, and particularly this recipe. It actually has a Mexican twist to it. Why it should have come from Spokane is anybody's guess, but try it, you'll like it.

SPOKANE PIZZA

1   pound lean ground beef
1   medium-size onion, chopped
1   teaspoon garlic salt
1   4-ounce can diced green chilies
½   cup chili sauce or ketchup
5   flour tortillas
2   tablespoons melted butter or margarine
1   16-ounce can refried beans
1   2¼-ounce can sliced ripe olives, drained
2   cups shredded mozzarella or jack cheese
½   cup grated Parmesan cheese
1   medium size firm ripe avocado, peeled, pitted, and sliced
     Taco sauce or green chili sauce
     Sour cream

In a wide frying pan over medium-high heat, crumble in the beef and cook until browned; stir in the onion and cook until the onion is limp. Add the garlic salt, green chilies, and chili sauce, and stir until well mixed. Set aside.

Brush the tortillas on both sides with melted butter and overlap them in a 14-inch pizza pan to cover the bottom. Broil about 3 inches below heat for 3 or 4 minutes or until lightly browned and crisp. Remove the pan from the broiler and set the oven temperature at 450°.

Spread the tortillas evenly with the beans, then spoon the meat mixture on top. Distribute the olives over the meat, then top with the shredded cheese and Parmesan. Bake on the lowest rack in a 450° oven for about 10 minutes or until the cheese is bubbly. Garnish with avocado slices, then cut into wedges to serve. Pass the taco sauce and sour cream to spoon over individual portions.

Serves 4 to 6.

A Name Change

It was at this time I decided to change my name. While looking through an English book, an old yellowed newspaper article fell to the floor. It was about a woman named Elinor Glynn, and as I read it I thought, "Gee, that's a neat way of spelling 'Eleanor.'"

Now, I'd never liked my name. The Mary was too plain and the Eleanor seemed stiff, and it was definitely too long. I wrote out "Elinor Donahue" and counted the letters— thirteen! That had been, my Mother told me, my lucky number. Good things often happened to me on the thirteenth of the month and especially on the Fridays.

That day I asked her if I could change my name and gave her my reasons. She said a resounding yes, as we could certainly use a change of luck by that time.

Don't you feel good when you make a decision and decide to go for it? We did.

This lemonade recipe was sent to me a few years ago. Thank you, Mary, wherever you are. It is a perfect drink for a pizza party.

Enjoying a candied apple.

LEMONADE

From the kitchen of Mary Spies

1	12-ounce can frozen orange juice
1	12-ounce can frozen lemonade
1	16-ounce bottle 7-Up or Teem

$1\frac{3}{4}$ cups sugar

In a large container mix all of the above ingredients and add enough water and ice to make 6 quarts.
Makes 6 quarts.

Here I am in a shoot for a one-time modeling job in MacArthur Park in Los Angeles.

At the dinner table in 1951, Margaret O'Brien (right) and I (left) were enemies and were supposed to be glaring at each other in Her First Romance, *but being good friends, we kept getting the giggles instead. The photographer just gave up and shot it anyway.*

RIVALS: Margaret O'Brien (left), and I are "rivals for the affections of Allen Martin in Columbia's The Romantic Age.*"*

Bad, Bleached, and Blonde

Coincidentally, not long after my name change, I was cast in *Her First Romance,* starring a now almost grown-up Margaret O'Brien. Instead of being her best friend, this time I played a nasty, snotty bad girl. To make me look more the part, my hair was bleached blonde, which I thought was the living end, and I kept it that way for at least two more years.

One of the scenes had Margaret in a spinach-eating contest, which in retrospect was pretty disgusting. Shaved ice cones all day long is one thing. Spinach all day is something else again.

That brings me to vegetables, which, at the time, were not widely enjoyed. Take eggplant, for instance. Today it is quite popular, and when I've made it, even those who profess to hate it, eat it and love it in this form.

EGGPLANT PROVENÇAL

1 large eggplant, cut in wedges (cut in half the long way and then each half in 3 or 4 wedges)
1 large onion, sliced thin

Sauce:
¾ large can tomato sauce
½ cup wine vinegar
1 cup sugar
½ cup water
¼ cup olive oil
½ head garlic, chopped
1 teaspoon basil
1 teaspoon oregano

Coarse salt and pepper to taste
1 cup Parmesan cheese

Preheat the oven to 400°. Put the eggplant in an oven-proof dish. Cover with thinly-sliced onion, and pour the sauce over. Bake for 1 to 1 hour and 15 minutes. When tender and done, sprinkle liberally with freshly grated Parmesan cheese while hot.

This is just delicious at room temperature or it can be served hot, whichever you prefer.

Serves 2 to 4.

Brother Comes Home

During this time my brother Dayod (Gerald) had returned from his duty in the Canadian Scottish Army, which he had crossed the American border to join in 1939. He had served six years in the front lines during the Second World War and had been hospitalized in Canada for multiple wounds, which he suffered with for many years. He later came to live with Mother and me.

Soon Dayod was able to send for his son, Geoffrey, who was born to his English wife, whom my brother had married while in England during the war. Now we had a little boy, too. Geoff was three, adorable, and frightened, and my mother took him to her heart.

Dayod had a difficult time adjusting to civilian life, but eventually he remarried and had a second child, a daughter named Marcia Ann.

Geoff, after his own struggles, is a fine young man and the father of two wonderful daughters, Elisha and Danielle.

Here's a recipe for a favorite English meal.

FISH AND CHIPS

8   4- to 6-ounce good quality fish fillets (cod, haddock, etc.)
Good quality vegetable oil for deep frying

Batter:
2   packages dry yeast
2½ cups milk (room temperature)
1   medium egg yolk
¾ cup all-purpose flour
¼ teaspoon baking powder
¾ cup cornstarch
   Pinch cayenne pepper
½ teaspoon soy sauce
   Salt to taste
   All-purpose flour

Chips:
   Potatoes (about 8 ounces per person)
   Good quality vegetable oil
   Salt

Dissolve the yeast in a little milk and leave it in a warm place to ferment.

In a large bowl mix together the milk, egg yolk, flour, baking powder, and cornstarch. Add the yeast mixture and seasonings. Cover and leave at room temperature for 1 to 2 hours until the mixture begins to ferment.

In a deep fryer or large saucepan heat the vegetable oil to 375° to 400°. Test the oil to make sure it is hot enough by dropping a little batter. Season and lightly flour the fish pieces, dip them in the batter, and fry them in the hot oil. Drain them and keep them warm in a 200° oven.

Peel and cut the potatoes into the desired sized pieces (somewhere between steak fries and wedges is good). Wash the chips, drain well on paper towels, and pat dry.

Heat the oil to 250° in a deep fryer. Fry the chips 2 or 3 handfuls at a time until soft but not colored. Remove from the oil and drain. At this point, you can store the chips in the refrigerator for a couple of days. To serve the chips, refry in oil heated to 350° to 400° until they are crisp.

Season lightly with salt and serve immediately.
Serves 4.

Geoff with me in Hollywood.

Down and Out in Beverly Hills

The years of 1950 and 1951 passed in a blur. Many things happened. Many changes occurred. We had to leave our beautiful house in Hollywood. After selling off some personal items, we moved to a small apartment on the eastern edge of Beverly Hills. Now the name Beverly Hills has cachet—big homes, big money. Not all of that particular postal designation is that way, believe me.

Mother secured a loan and paid Mrs. Long my back tuition, and in exchange I was given a high school diploma. I had actually completed, sort of, the eighth grade.

I had one job in that period (again as a blonde), a small part with Elizabeth Taylor in *Love Is Better Than Ever,* but mother returned to work, this time in the basement of the May Company as a gift wrapper.

There wasn't much money for groceries, and sometimes it looked as though the cupboards were bare. But mother could always come up with something out of what seemed like nothing. Hence, the following recipe.

MOTHER HUBBARD'S VEGGIE STEW

The funny thing about this is that some years later, when I was working a long day on Father Knows Best, *Mother called the set to see what I might like for dinner. I asked for vegetable stew and had to describe it to her. She had blocked memories of those times right out. But she made it that night, and while I didn't say anything, she looked at me with her eyes glistening. "It isn't the same, is it, honey?"*

"No, Mother, I said, "it's delicious, but that's because you don't have *to make it now. Isn't that nice?"*

2   potatoes, quartered
4   carrots, cut in large chunks
4   ribs celery, cut in large chunks
1   large onion, quartered
1   10¾-ounce can chicken broth
2   tablespoons all-purpose flour

Optional:
1   handful of frozen peas
1   14-ounce can niblets corn, drained
    Basil
    Marjoram
    Salt and pepper to taste

In a skillet combine the potatoes, carrots, celery, and onion. Add the broth. Bring to a boil, cover, and reduce the heat to a simmer. Cook for 30 to 40 minutes until fork tender. Add the peas or corn at this point. Remove some of the broth to mix with the flour and blend until smooth. Return the flour mixture to the skillet. Cook to thicken. Season with salt and pepper to taste. Of course, you can add basil or marjoram or anything else you fancy.
Serves 2.

Ballet lessons: Mary Eleanor makes a pointe and pirouettes into Elinor.

Young and Hungry

During this strange period, I spent a lot of time alone. Mother began working at night, too, for a costumer in Hollywood named Christine. She and Mother sewed some of the first costumes for Disneyland before it opened in 1955.

Being young and hungry all the time, I had to learn to cook, and since I loved eggs, they were it—scrambled, puffy omelettes, egg salad, and my favorite, stuffed eggs.

Taking a break during ballet lessons.

STUFFED EGGS

Hard boil the eggs (gently, don't overcook) and let cool.

Peel and halve, putting the yolks in a bowl; set the whites on an egg plate or dish.

Mash the yolks with mayonnaise (homemade if you like), a bit of yellow mustard, and sweet or bread-and-butter pickles, chopped. Season with celery salt (not too much), a dash of paprika, and a wee dash of cayenne.

Fill the egg whites with the yolk mixture, prettily, and top with a light sprinkling of paprika or a tiny slice of pickle.

Joining the Chorus Line

One day, while walking with Mother to her day job at the May Company, we ran right into Carlos Romero, the man who'd choreographed the dances in *Love Is Better Than Ever.*

He greeted us warmly and asked how things were going for us.

"Not too well," Mother said, "but we're doing all right."

"How would she like to dance in the chorus? She's tall enough, and her age shouldn't be a problem," Romero asked.

She looked at me, and I looked at her. What did I know about being in a chorus line? But dancing is dancing, so I said, "Yes, I'll try it." I did, and the next two years were about the most fun I'd had in a long time.

Whenever there was a little money, we would go to Smokey Joe's, a barbecue place near where I still took dance lessons (on scholarship, I might add; otherwise, we couldn't have managed it).

They made the best cole slaw ever at Smokey Joe's, and finally a few years ago their recipe was printed in a newspaper. I'm happy to present it to you.

This shot from a modeling job was screened on the inside of men's ties later in the 1950s. It infuriated Gene Rodney, the producer of Father Knows Best—*especially when Mother and I gave them to the crew as joke Christmas presents after seeing them on sale in a seedy shop on Hollywood Boulevard.*

P.S. My husband, Lou, has one that I'd saved!

SMOKEY JOE'S PINEAPPLE COLE SLAW

1	to 2 tablespoons sugar
1	8-ounce can crushed pineapple, undrained
2	dashes ground nutmeg
2	dashes ground cinnamon
1	cup sour cream, chilled
2	cups finely shredded red cabbage
2	cups finely shredded white cabbage

In a saucepan combine the sugar and pineapple, and simmer uncovered for 5 minutes or until as thick as drained pineapple. Add the nutmeg and cinnamon, and cool. Add the sour cream and blend well. Chill.

When ready to serve, in a salad bowl combine the cabbages, pour the dressing over the cabbages, and toss to coat well. *Makes about 5 cups.*

Another sultry pose of the young chorine.

Dancing Fool

I was added to Romero's line of dancers, a few of whom were as young as I, to rehearse for a big show, actually two shows, on different nights for a General Electric convention in San Francisco.

I took to chorus work like a duck to water, and, except for a couple of girls who'd been baby chorus dancers in *Unfinished Dance,* everyone was very welcoming to me. Even those other girls quickly came around.

This show was Frank Sinatra's return to performing after a mysterious loss of voice that he had suffered. The producers didn't know what to expect and were nervous. But when Frank took the microphone, magic happened, as it had in the past. His voice was even richer and warmer than it had ever been. He brought the house down.

Later on, I became a Morro-Landis dancer and did the Los Angeles Police Show for two years running, as well as other shows for them.

One girl's mother would bring in banana bread from time to time. It was before anyone talked about carbohydrate loading, but the mother felt it was good for us when we were dancing so hard.

BANANA BREAD

2   cups mashed bananas
3   eggs
1   cup oil
1   teaspoon vanilla extract
2   cups all-purpose flour
1   cup sugar
1   teaspoon baking soda
¼   teaspoon salt

Preheat the oven to 350°. In a large bowl combine the bananas, eggs, oil, and vanilla, and mix well. Sift together the flour, sugar, soda, and salt and add to banana mixture. Pour the batter into a waxed paper lined 5 x 9-inch loaf pan. Bake for 50 minutes or until done.
Makes 1 loaf.

Tap Billing

During my chorus years, I occasionally worked on the bill with the Will Mastin Trio, a family of three brothers who sang and danced. Mr. Mastin, the leader of the group, was giving his nephew a start in his young career. The nephew was a great tap dancer, the best I'd ever seen. And he did fabulous impersonations and sang like an angel.

Their billing was:

The Will Mastin Trio
with Sammy Davis, Jr.

The next time I worked with them, Sammy's letters were bigger and said "and Sammy Davis, Jr."
 The year after that, it was:

Sammy Davis, Jr. and The Will Mastin Trio

Sammy Davis, Jr.

The last I saw of the act, it was:

Sammy Davis, Jr.
with The Will Mastin Trio

Sammy was a great guy and a superior talent. His widow, Altovise Davis, shared this with me:
 "I love fish—any kind—and Sammy would make this shrimp and rice thing," she told me. "He was half Spanish, you know. His mother was Spanish. And he'd make this very hot and spicy because I just love hot sauce—Tabasco—lots of it!"
 Alto and I have known each other for more than twenty years (we're both members of Share, Inc., and there's a photograph of us dancing in a show later in this book), and a kinder, nicer lady would be hard to find.

ALTOVISE AND SAMMY'S SHRIMP SASSY

2   tablespoons butter
2   or 3 green onions, white and tops,
      diagonally sliced
1   sprig parsley, chopped
1½ cups rice
3   cups water
1   tablespoon slivered almonds

2   tablespoons butter
½   green bell pepper, thinly sliced
½   yellow bell pepper, thinly sliced
½   bright red bell pepper, thinly sliced
1   green onion, white and top, sliced
1   clove garlic, minced
½   teaspoon hot pepper sauce
      Dash chili powder
½   cup fresh pea pods
½   teaspoon cornstarch
1   pound shrimp, peeled, deveined, and
      rinsed
1   large ripe tomato, chopped
¼   cup water

In a skillet melt 2 tablespoons of butter and sauté the onions until tender but not brown. In a saucepan combine the rice and water. Add the parsley and onions, cover, and simmer for about 30 minutes.

Remove the cover, fluff the rice with a fork, and add the slivered almonds.

In a large pan melt 2 tablespoons of butter and sauté the peppers, onion, and garlic until tender. Add the pepper sauce, chili powder, pea pods, cornstarch, and uncooked shrimp. Add the chopped tomatoes, and stir. Add ¼ cup of water. Cover and simmer about 10 minutes until the shrimp is done. It cooks quickly. Toss lightly once or twice while cooking.

Uncover and let the Sassy steam for a few minutes. Serve over the hot rice pilaf. *Serves 6.*

Exotic Dancer

We went for our costumes to a woman named Mme. Houda in downtown Los Angeles. She handled the big circuses and huge tent shows, and we were fitted in the most exotic costumes I'd ever seen. As one girl's mother said, "Why, they're no more than two beads and a pearl." But by today's standards they were quite chaste and totally covered us up.

This recipe, so very simple to prepare, has an exotic feeling to it. Served with plain or fried rice and snow peas, you'll have a lovely meal in a jiffy.

SHRIMP HAWAII

2   tablespoons salad oil
1   pound raw shrimp, shelled and
        deveined
2   green onions, cut into 2-inch lengths
2   teaspoons sugar
½   teaspoon salt
1   tablespoon soy sauce
2   teaspoons toasted sesame seeds

In a heavy pan heat the oil over high heat.
Add the shrimp, onions, sugar, salt, and soy
sauce. Cook, stirring constantly, for 7 to 8
minutes until the shrimp are tender. Do not
overcook. Sprinkle with toasted sesame seeds
and serve.
Serves 2 to 4.

*At age sixteen, I performed for the second year in the Los Angeles County
Police Show. On the same bill were such stars as Liberace, Frank Sinatra,
the Marx Brothers, The Modernaires, and various variety acts. Groucho
and Harpo were very nice. Chico was a flirt. Enough said.*

Hungry

Getting back to the G.E. Convention shows... When we all left for San Francisco on the train, my
mother gave me ten dollars for food for the five days that I would be away. It was all she could
spare, and she warned me to be cautious about how I spent it. When I got home I returned to
her six dollars.

"How did you do that?" she asked with horror.

"Oh, it was easy," I replied. Of course, I was about five pounds lighter, but so what.

All week I'd eaten at the same cafeteria and averaged spending about eighty-five cents a
day—this was 1951, remember. I was doing fine until Friday night, the night of our big finale
show.

It was banquet style and the performances went on while the audience dined. After we'd finished, the waiters cleared the main course off the tables onto trays to be taken to the kitchen. A
couple of us spied the plates piled with leftover food. A waiter saw us eyeing the food and asked
if we were hungry. When we nodded yes, he told us to stay right where we were. He came back
with fresh plates for each of us, and we filled up.

The feature of each plate was a Cornish game hen stuffed with wild rice, and when I found
this recipe some years ago, it brought back those wonderful memories of the music, the costumes, and that oh-so-kind waiter.

CORNISH HEN AND WILD RICE SUPREME

4   fresh or frozen Cornish game hens
2   tablespoons butter, melted
1   6-ounce package long grain and wild
     rice mix
1   10¾-ounce can chicken broth
2   tablespoons butter (again)
1   bunch green onions, sliced
6   large mushrooms, sliced
½   cup dry white wine
2   bay leaves

Thaw the hens, if frozen. Remove the giblets. Rinse and pat dry. Brush inside and out with 1 tablespoon of melted butter. Remove the seasoning packet from the rice mix. Use 1 teaspoon per hen, rubbing inside and out. Place the hens breast up in a shallow roasting pan. Truss if desired. Pour the chicken broth and ½ cup of water into the pan. Bake at 450° for 15 minutes.

Meanwhile, in a skillet melt 2 tablespoons of butter. Add the green onions, mushrooms, and rice packet from the mix. Sauté, stirring frequently. Slowly add 1¼ cups of water, the remaining seasoning from the rice mix, wine, and the bay leaves. Bring to a boil. Pour the rice mixture into the roasting pan, making sure the rice does not rest on top of the hens. Brush the hens with the remaining butter. Cover loosely with foil. Reduce the oven temperature to 350° and bake an additional 45 minutes or until all the liquid is absorbed. Discard the bay leaves. Serve the hens on a bed of the rice. *Serves 4.*

Another shot of the Los Angeles County Police Department Show from the Shrine Auditorium. One of my best friends at the time was Tina Jankowski (that's her kneeling in front of me).

Skirting the Issue

I was also on the same bill with Liberace for one of the Police Shows. He was a sweet, dear man. His brother George conducted for him, and Liberace let George do all of the directing. The chorus dressing rooms were under the stage and when Liberace was on stage, we had to go down and make a costume change. He pounded his left foot in time to his music while he played, and as we went below, we could hear him banging away as though he'd nearly come through the floor. He took such joy in his music that it was contagious.

One guest star was Christine Jorgensen, who had just had the first sex-change operation. I don't know why she was on the bill, but there she was, right after one of our big dance numbers.

I had the misfortune of losing my skirt—a big fluffy ballet-like thing—near

WEARING MY "AIR ELLIE" PUMPS—Some high-flying footwork, I'd say, as Ray Bolger and I cut a rug.

the end of a specialty bit. (My male dance partner had squeezed my waist on a "lift" and unhooked it.) There was nothing to do but leave it there, but with a very quick wit, Miss Jorgensen made a cute joke of it, and carried it into the wings—getting a huge laugh from the audience. I was asked to repeat my boo-boo for the rest of the show's run, but I politely declined.

This is a new soup I just made. It's healthful and I think it tastes great and is nice for a change of pace.

CABBAGE VEGETABLE SOUP

1   medium head cabbage
6   carrots
1   large onion
2   green bell peppers
1   28-ounce can chopped Italian tomatoes, undrained
2   14½-ounce cans beef broth (Swanson's)
    Water
1   package Lipton Onion Soup Mix
1   teaspoon basil
1   large bay leaf
    Salt and freshly ground pepper to taste
1   cup fresh green beans
½   cup frozen petit peas
½   cup frozen corn niblets
1   cup large elbow macaroni

Chop all of the fresh vegetables. Set the green beans aside. In a large soup pot or Dutch oven combine the cabbage, carrots, onion, and bell pepper. Add the canned tomatoes, broth, water, and onion soup mix, and stir together. Add the basil, bay leaf, salt, and pepper, and incorporate. Bring all to a boil and cook for 10 minutes, and then simmer. After 20 minutes, add the green beans and cook until all are tender —approximately 30 minutes or to your liking (see Note). Turn off the heat and let it rest.

In a separate pot cook the macaroni in boiling salted water for not more than 5 minutes. Drain well and add to the pot. Just before reheating, add the peas and corn directly from the frozen packages. Adjust the seasonings. Reheat.

Note: Normally, I prefer vegetables in the more up-to-date fashion—full color and al dente. However this soup is best when cooked more for the flavors to fully blend. Also, canned vegetable broth can be substituted for beef broth for vegetarians.
Serves 10 to 12.

Testing with the Scarecrow

While still dancing in the chorus, I'd occasionally get a TV job. The medium was relatively new then, and most of the shows were put on film unless they were broadcast live, which was a whole other ball of wax. Trapeze work without a net was what that was.

Anyway, one show I loved doing was *The Ray Bolger Show.* He was a delightful man, and my dance audition for him was very unusual. Of course I had a number prepared, and I was so nervous. But after we were introduced, he said to his pianist, "Play something, Morty." We faced each other and started dancing. Just listening to the music and the rhythms, we were tapping away in counter-point. His eyes lit up—he smiled—and I had the job.

The Ray Bolger Show was the first time I worked with Betty Lynn, a young movie actress from Fox Studios who went on to fame as Thelma Lou, Barney's girlfriend, on *The Andy Griffith Show.* She's a funny, bright, and loving lady, and she wants to share this with you.

BETTY LYNN'S CAN'T BE BEET SALAD

1   6-ounce box cherry gelatin
1   20-ounce can shoestring beets, drained
1   7½-ounce package slivered almonds
    Lettuce leaves
    Mayonnaise/sour cream

Make the gelatin as directed for additions. Add the drained beets and almonds. Pour into a loaf pan or small molds. Chill until firm. Unmold and slice, if in a loaf pan, and place on lettuce leaves.

In a small bowl combine equal amounts of mayonnaise and sour cream. Spoon a dollop of the dressing mixture on each serving.
Serves 4 to 6.

Ray Bolger, the Scarecrow from The Wizard of Oz, *and I compete in a dancing contest on his television show, while Betty Lynn twirls away with her partner at left.*

Something's Fishy

Once, while dancing in the annual Los Angeles County Police Show, we worked with an act called "Captain Winston and His Seals." Now the headliners were big stars (the Marx Brothers, Jack Benny, and a young Liberace), but on the remainder of the bill were variety acts from clubs or vaudeville.

The show that year had a Parisian theme, and we girls had completed a portion of a number with beach balls and singing about St. Tropez. We were to place ourselves seated on stage, while Captain Winston did his thing with his charges.

Darling and clever seals may be, but they ate a lot of fish on stage. There were fish in the Captain's pockets, and the seals had mackerel breath. Unknown to us, one of the young married dancers was in the early stages of pregnancy, and as the act proceeded, she started crawling off-stage into the wings and looking a bit pale around the edges. As she passed me, she hissed, "Shh—I'll be back."

After the seals finished their act, she trotted back on stage to her position with a big smile on her face and we finished the number. No one in the audience ever knew anything had gone differently.

This is one of my all-time favorite pasta dishes, and it seems somewhat appropriate here, though it smells wonderful while cooking and tastes even better.

How do you like our Roman centurion outfits for the Los Angeles County Police Show?

WHITE CLAM SAUCE WITH LINGUINI

½ cup butter or margarine
¼ cup olive oil
2 cloves garlic, minced
2 7½-ounce cans of minced clams
Bottled clam juice
Salt
Pepper
8 ounces linguini

In a saucepan heat the butter and oil and sauté the garlic and cook until golden. Drain the clams, reserve the liquid, and add enough clam juice to the liquid to make 2 cups. Stir the liquid into the butter mixture and simmer, uncovered, for 10 minutes. Add the clams, parsley, and salt and pepper to taste. Cook until heated thoroughly.

Meanwhile, in a separate pot cook the linguini in boiling salted water until tender and drain. Serve the sauce over hot linguini. *Serves 4.*

Father Knows Best, and So Does Andy Griffith

The Best Advice

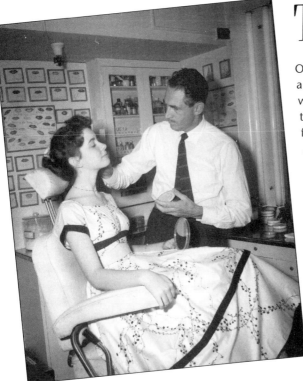

Clay Campbell, the head of the Columbia Pictures makeup department, prepares me to be a TV Princess.

One day when I was sixteen, I got a call from a manager who believed in me. Her name was Lillie Messinger, and without her I certainly wouldn't be writing this book, for she forced me to go on an interview for *Father Knows Best.*

I was to audition for Eugene B. Rodney, Robert Young's partner, and I said I couldn't go because my hair was wet and it would take too long to go in the bus to the office on Sunset Boulevard, and on and on I made excuses. "Go!" Miss Messinger said. I went. Rodney didn't like me. I looked too young and ordinary.

So Miss Messinger made another appointment for me and got me all dolled up. She even drove me there in her Jaguar. Rodney still didn't like me. I looked too old and worldly wise.

Miss Messinger pestered Rodney for several weeks to see me yet again, when they struck a deal. If he would test me on film, she would promise to leave him alone.

I tested with Robert Young, and after dissolving in nervous tears on my first try, we finally completed a take.

I was mortified when we left the studio and asked Mother not to ask me how it went or to ever mention it again.

Six weeks later I found out I had the part.

This certainly called for a celebration, so Mother and I went to a seafood place near our apartment, and I had crab cakes for the first time. They are still a huge favorite of mine.

CRAB CAKES

2½ cups lump crab meat (about 1 pound)
2   cups fine fresh bread crumbs
2   eggs, well beaten
1   tablespoon Dijon-style mustard
½   teaspoon Worcestershire sauce
2   tablespoons finely chopped parsley
¼   cup finely chopped green onions
1   teaspoon Old Bay seasoning
½   cup mayonnaise
    Corn, peanut or vegetable oil
    Lemon wedges
    Tartar sauce

In a mixing bowl combine the crab meat in and 1½ cups of the bread crumbs, eggs, mustard, Worcestershire sauce, parsley, onions, seasoning, and mayonnaise. Blend, leaving the crab lumps as whole as possible.

Shape the mixture into 10 portions of equal size. Shape into flat patties.

Coat each portion with the remaining bread crumbs. Chill until ready to cook.

In a heavy skillet heat 2 tablespoons of oil on medium high. Add a few cakes at a time (do not crowd) and cook for 2 to 2½ minutes per side until golden brown on both sides.

Drain on paper towels. Serve with the lemon wedges and tartar sauce.
Makes 10.

My TV Mom

Jane Wyatt, who played my mother on *Father Knows Best,* said about the pilot episode we shot, "You and Billy were awfully good, but I just hated myself. I don't know what I thought I was playing. My face never changed and those clothes. I looked like I was going to take a stroll on the boulevard, much too dressed up in those tight skirts."

I love her so, and we have remained pals all these years.

She doesn't do much cooking—never did—but she gave me this recipe that belonged to her great-grandmother.

Coming out of Stage 11 with my TV mother and father, Jane Wyatt and Robert Young.

GREAT-GRANDMOTHER'S RICE PUDDING

1   quart milk
9   teaspoons rice
9   teaspoons sugar
2   teaspoons vanilla extract

In a casserole dish combine all of the ingredients. Bake at 325° for 2 hours.

This will reduce by about half and have a black skin on top.

Serves 4 to 6.

That's not Trigger and I'm not a horsewoman, but I was truly in love with my first pair of blue jeans at age sixteen. How about that plaid shirt and bolo tie!

A Teen in Blue Jeans

With all the hustle and bustle of being on a network TV series, I really was a normal teenager, at least in one respect. When I did *The Ray Bolger Show,* they bought me blue jeans and a plaid shirt to wear. Now my mother had never allowed me to wear jeans. I was so tickled to be dressed like every other teenager that the producer gave them to me when I finished work. What could Mother say?

After I started work on *Father Knows Best,* I wore those same clothes on the buses I took to the studio. Mother couldn't get them away from me. Couldn't she please wash them on Sunday? No, they were not dirty. After all, I only wore them to work and then to come home—until they began to stand up on their own. Then I conceded that they might need laundering.

Around the corner from where we shot at Columbia Studios in Hollywood was a funny, tacky little bar-like place that served great hamburgers, the real '50s kind—juicy and greasy.

This was their premier burger.

PEANUT-BACON CHEESEBURGER

1   **pound ground beef**
4   **slices Cheddar cheese**
4   **hamburger buns, lightly toasted**
4   **tablespoons chopped, salted peanuts**
8   **slices bacon, cooked crisp**
4   **thin slices red onion**

Fry the 4 meat patties. On the top side place the cheese slices; put each patty on the bottom of a toasted bun, and sprinkle 1 tablespoon of chopped peanuts on each patty. Top with bacon. If you want the onion and you think you can get your mouth around it, go ahead. Spread mustard or any condiment of your choice on the top bun. That's it.

Serves 4.

Finding the Right Direction

A little background for those who enjoy TV history and statistics: *Father Knows Best* made its debut in 1949 as an NBC Radio series starring Robert Young. When the radio show made its move to television on October 3, 1954, on CBS-TV in the 10 P.M. (Eastern) Sunday time slot, Mr. Young was the only member of the radio cast who stayed with the show.

CBS canceled us after only one season, in March of 1955, but there was such a deluge of viewer mail that NBC decided we were worth a shot, so from the fall of 1956 until the summer of 1958 we were on NBC at 8:30 P.M. Wednesdays. The reason NBC moved us up from the 10 o'clock slot was so the whole family could watch our show about one of America's most wholesome families, the Andersons of Springfield, a typical Midwestern town.

In fall of 1958, CBS decided they wanted us back, so we switched from NBC to CBS from 1958 through 1960 at 8:30 P.M. Mondays. We quit making episodes in 1960. (At that time we were the Number 6 show in the Top 10 of the Nielsen ratings.) The show ran in reruns during prime time on CBS in 1960, 1961, and 1962, and then ABC carried the reruns in prime time during the winter of 1962-63, which made us one of the few shows ever to air in prime time on all three major television networks.

One other interesting sidelight: We made a short film for the U.S. Treasury Department in 1959 to help promote their U.S. Savings Bond drive. The film never aired on TV but was screened in schools, churches, and civic organizations.

Anyway, the director of *Father Knows Best* for the first two seasons was William "Bill" Russell. He was a great, jolly bear of a man, always fun on the set. He launched the popularity of the series with his energetic direction.

For instance, when filming a scene, once the master (or whole scene) is shot, the camera is reset for closeups. The other actor then stands off-camera and gives his or her lines to the one

Director William Russell gives some pointers to Robert Easton and me just before the camera rolls in a 1955 Father Knows Best *episode titled "Betty Hates Carter."*

being filmed. If one was unfortunate enough to have the position next to Mr. Russell when he yelled "Action!," you might suffer a mild loss of hearing for the next few minutes. Other than that, he was perfect. His nickname for me was "Miss Duse," for Eleanora Duse, a nineteenth-century stage actress.

Mr. Russell loved his food and had a big appetite, and he adored sweets. This gelatin salad was very popular in the 1950s.

LIME GELATIN SALAD

1 8¼-ounce can crushed pineapple in own juice
1 3-ounce package lime gelatin
2 3-ounce packages Philadelphia cream cheese
1 8-ounce carton whipping cream
2 little cans half and half

In a saucepan heat the pineapple to boiling (do not drain). Dissolve the gelatin in the pineapple. Let cool.

In a large bowl combine the softened cream cheese and a little half and half, and beat until smooth. Whip the cream. Mix the whole thing together and pour into a mold or in sherbet glasses. Refrigerate.
Serves 4 to 6.

UCLA Night School

The schoolteacher on the set was Lillian Barkley. She had been the head teacher at Columbia Pictures Studios for years and we were lucky to have her.

Lauren Chapin, who played my little sister, and Billy Gray, who played my brother, did their three hours every day, but Miss Barkley was appalled when she heard the story of my schooling.

After discussing it with Mother, she convinced me to take some classes through her alma mater, UCLA. I was terrified to try—fearful that I could never pass the entrance exam. So Miss Barkley arranged

Billy Gray, Lauren Chapin, and I do our homework for Miss Barkley.

for me to take a correspondence course through Los Angeles City College in lieu of the exam, and I passed. I then began taking as much of a class load as I could manage and still work all day, every day, too.

I even took an on-campus class one night a week, which Miss Barkley fought the school on like a tiger. The class was first-year acting and she didn't think I should have to take a beginner's course! However, I learned a lot while there and was very glad I'd gone.

There was a small cafe next to our stage (there always is, isn't there!), and when any of us were under the weather, Miss Barkley would go next door and get either a pot of peppermint tea, if you had a stomach ache, or chamomile for a cold, and sometimes cinnamon toast. Whenever I'm very tired or achy, that is what I crave.

Back to school days for Lauren Chapin, Billy Gray, me, Jane Wyatt, and Robert Young.

Piano practice.

TEA AND TOAST

Select a tea of your choice, put boiling hot water in a pot, throw out the water, then add your tea and more boiling water. Steep until it's the desired strength.

Toast white or wheat bread. While warm, butter well with softened butter, sprinkle liberally with granulated or confectioners' sugar (my mother's choice), and then sprinkle with cinnamon.

I like lots; others might like less. Cut the slices in half and feel pampered.

Father's Favorite

I couldn't play piano or read music, I couldn't play tennis, and I definitely couldn't fence. But being a normal teenager, I sure could talk on the telephone.

One of Robert Young's four daughters, Betty Lou, was a good friend. She often came with her sisters Carol Ann, Barbara, and Kathy to the set.

Betty Lou kindly sent this recipe, which was her Dad's favorite Sunday dinner, from her home in the Southwest where she lives with her husband, John Gleason. She has pared it down to meet today's health-conscious standards, but feel free to add back such embellishments as leeks, bacon, corn, etc.

En garde! Eat your heart out, Errol Flynn!

ROBERT YOUNG'S FAVORITE CREAMY CLAM CHOWDER

1¼ cups peeled, diced potatoes
½   cup water
⅓   cup chopped celery
⅓   chopped onion
1   tablespoon reduced-calorie margarine
1   12-ounce can evaporated skim milk
1   cup skim milk
1   tablespoon cornstarch
1   10-ounce can whole shelled clams,
       drained (discarding the clam juice
       lowers the sodium level)
¼   teaspoon salt
⅛   teaspoon ground white pepper

In a Dutch oven combine the potato, water, celery, onion, and margarine. Place over medium-high heat, and bring to a boil. Cover, reduce the heat, and simmer for 15 minutes or until the potatoes are tender.

In a small bowl combine the evaporated skim milk, skim milk, and cornstarch. Add the milk mixture to the potato mixture. Add the clams, salt, and pepper. Cover over medium heat, stirring constantly, for 10 minutes or until thickened and bubbly. Ladle the chowder into individual bowls, and serve with water crackers, if desired.

Note: Reduce the calories, fat, and cholesterol in cream-based soups by using skim or low-fat milk in place of whipping cream or half and half. Another way to lighten cream soups while keeping the characteristic smooth, velvety texture, is to use puréed vegetables in place of cream.

Makes 5 cups (about 176 calories per 1-cup serving).

How about a match?

Now this was something I excelled at as a teenager.

Making A Date

Robert Easton, who played one of my boyfriends on *Father Knows Best,* is now known as "the Henry Higgins of Hollywood" for his work as a dialect coach to actors for film and television. We actually had a couple of movie dates, chaperoned by his mother who drove the car. He continues to act occasionally in feature films. Many thanks to him for these recipes. They are unique indeed.

Robert Easton adopts a casual attitude toward women as Cindy Robbins and I seem very interested in him in the "Betty Hates Carter" episode of Father Knows Best.

EASTON'S TUNA CASSEROLE SURPRISE

1   12-ounce can tuna, packed in water
    not oil
1   10¾-ounce can mushroom or cream
    of chicken soup
1   15-ounce can peas (petit pois)
1   6-ounce can mushrooms
    Water (to make it as thick or thin as
    you wish)

Rice, wheat, or corn Chex cereal

In a large bowl combine the tuna, mushroom soup, peas, mushrooms, and water. Microwave on high for about 5 minutes. Serve over Rice Chex (or Wheat Chex or Corn Chex).
Serves 2 to 4.

EASTON'S OPEN-FACED SANDWICH SUPREME

Raisin walnut bread
Liver sausage
Seedless green grapes

Cover the bread with sausage and then embed with grapes. This can be topped with yogurt or sour cream.

Eating Habits

Robert Young had very definite ideas about food. Before he passed away on July 21, 1998, I was told, "He will not eat anything 'by hand.' Not sandwiches, not pizza, not even a cookie.

"And he is 'The World's Slowest Eater.'

"He cares not a whit if the food turns cold. He prefers it that way. He doesn't believe in calories; they're nonsense to him. The same with cholesterol. He eats what he wants and as much as he wants—and leaves what he doesn't want." So there.

I have always adored him. The following was one of his most favorite things to eat in the whole wide world.

Robert Young: My favorite TV father.

LIVER AND ONIONS WITH BACON

1. Cook 4 or more slices of bacon slowly, until crisp. Drain and save the drippings.

2. In 2 tablespoons of the drippings (or butter), slowly sauté 3 thinly sliced onions for about 20 minutes. They will cook way down.

3. Push to the side of the pan. Cut 1 pound of calf liver in ¼-inch thick slices, and sprinkle both sides of each slice with flour seasoned with salt and pepper. Add 2 tablespoons of bacon fat or butter to the pan and cook the liver quickly on both sides, turning once. Sprinkle the liver and onion with 2 tablespoons of vinegar. Cover the pan quickly and remove from the heat. Let stand alone 2 minutes.

Stir and serve immediately. Place bacon along side or, as Mr. Young preferred, crumbled on top.

Good Advice

Josephine was our wardrobe mistress. She'd been at Columbia for years and years. (She was the widow of Joseph Jefferson, a prominent actor of the legitimate theater in his day.) She treated all of us lovingly but wouldn't hesitate to tell me I was "getting too big for my britches" if I stepped out of line. And I'm sure I did more often than I care to remember.

She was very motherly, and I'm sure she'd like this recipe for Oven-Fried Chicken.

Josephine makes an adjustment on my dress before an early episode of Father Knows Best.

OVEN-FRIED CHICKEN

1	fresh chicken, cut in 8 pieces
¼	cup all-purpose flour
1½	teaspoons salt
1	teaspoon paprika
¼	teaspoon pepper
2	tablespoons solid shortening

Preheat the oven to 375°. Put the flour, salt, paprika, and pepper in a paper bag and "flour" the chicken pieces by shaking 1 or 2 at a time.

In a heavy skillet heat the shortening over medium-high heat. Brown the chicken pieces on both sides a few pieces at a time (do not crowd). When all are browned, drain off the accumulated fat, return the chicken to the pan, and bake for 35 minutes or until done and there is no pink near the bone. *Serves 4.*

My TV Brother

Bill (once upon a time Billy) Gray and I had a weird relationship on the set as brother and sister. Part flirtatious, part antagonistic, we have remained solid friends through the years.

He was and is a superior actor, and his body of work before *Father Knows Best* was formidable. He was fabulous in the sci-fi classic *The Day the Earth Stood Still,* with Michael Rennie and Patricia Neal (and Frances Bavier, Mayberry's Aunt Bee), and he was natural and funny in a series of Doris Day features, such as *By the Light of the Silvery Moon,* as well as many other movies.

When I asked him recently for a recipe for this book, he seemed taken aback for a moment and then without hesitation he described his mother's pancakes.

"Really light, you know, thin. You could wrap something in them, but I first had them with butter and syrup. They were really special."

What they sound like to me are Swedish pancakes, Bill. I hope you approve.

My TV brother Billy Gray and me—all jazzed up.

SWEDISH PANCAKES

2¼ **cups all-purpose flour**
2 **tablespoons sugar**
1 **teaspoon salt**
4 **cups milk**
7 **eggs**
   Butter or margarine
   Lingonberries and confectioners'
     sugar for topping

In a large bowl stir together the flour, sugar, and salt. Gradually add the milk while beating with a wire whisk until smooth. Add the eggs one a time and beat with a whisk after each addition. Let the batter stand for 30 minutes. Stir once more before cooking.

Grease a 9-inch skillet with butter or margarine and heat over medium heat. Pour ⅓ cup of the batter into the hot skillet. Roll the skillet to spread the batter evenly over the bottom of the skillet. Cook until the bottom is golden brown and the top is beginning to bubble. Using a spatula, carefully flip the pancake and continue to cook it until golden brown. Carefully roll the pancake and transfer it to serving plate. Keep warm in a 200° oven.

Top with lingonberries and confectioners' sugar and serve with butter. Instead of lingonberries, any fruit topping or syrup can be used.
Serves 6.

Designer Jean-Louis and I check out one of his creations.

Designing Man

Jean-Louis was the designer of clothes for Columbia. He also did all of Loretta Young's gowns for her, and he designed the notorious "nude" evening gown for Marlene Dietrich. In fact, while it was a work in progress, the gown was hanging in one of his mirrored dressing rooms, and Dietrich's high-heeled sandals were on the floor. Since no one was looking, I slipped off my flats and into her heels. What a thrill.

Jean-Louis also had a thriving couture business as well as a line of expensive ready-to-wear clothes that was sold in only the finest stores. Later in life, he married Loretta Young, and they lived happily in Palm Springs, California, until his death in 1997.

He was very helpful to me when his expertise in hiding figure faults came into play. More about that later, but now to honor his French heritage, I would like to offer this recipe.

POULET À LA NIVERNAIS
(Chicken Braised in Red Wine)

7	tablespoons butter
1	large onion, chopped
1	3-pound chicken in 8 pieces
4	carrots, sliced
½	pound eggplant, peeled and diced
2	tablespoons all-purpose flour
1	cup water
1½	cups red wine
	Salt and pepper
	Herbal bouquet (parsley, bay leaf, and thyme)

In a skillet heat half of the butter and brown the onion and chicken over medium-high heat. Put the chicken and onion into a casserole and save. To the skillet add the carrots and eggplant, and sauté for 8 to 10 minutes Place them in the casserole. In the same skillet melt the rest of the butter, blend the flour, and cook for 1 minute. Gradually add the water and bring all to a boil. Remove from heat and add the wine, salt, pepper, and bouquet. Blend well, and then pour into the casserole. Cover and simmer over low heat for 45 minutes or until the chicken is tender.
Serves 4 to 6.

Little Sister

Lauren Chapin, who played my little sister on *Father Knows Best,* and Billy got along great, but because I was such a "pill," they would gang up on me, which is what I deserved, and, of course, that only made it worse.

Jane Wyatt would have no problem getting us to stop bickering. She'd just say "Stop it! Right now!" and we would—for a second or two. Sometimes we three would kick under the table at one another or pinch if we were standing close together.

No matter how bothersome we were, Robert Young would never say anything. He'd just stand up, straighten himself, and silently and slowly leave the set. Then we knew we were really in trouble, with a capital T.

Lauren Chapin.

Lauren and I are good buddies these days, and I'm very proud of her in overcoming some difficulties in her young adulthood that many, without her strength and belief in God, have not accomplished as well.

This is a recipe straight from her kitchen to yours.

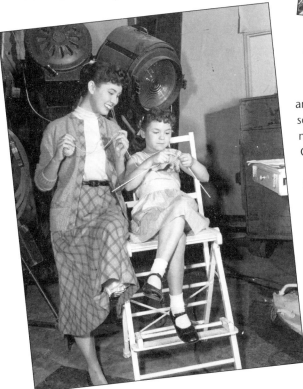

This is one of the rare peaceful moments between me and Lauren Chapin, my kid sister on Father Knows Best. *She was a normal energetic little girl, and I was the quintessential "only child." Sometimes it's hard learning to share.*

RAW APPLE CAKE

3   eggs
2   cups sugar
1½ cups oil
3   cups all-purpose flour
1   teaspoon baking soda
1   teaspoon salt
1   teaspoon ground cinnamon
1   teaspoon vanilla extract
3   cups raw chopped apples
1   cup pecans
      Confectioners' sugar

In a large bowl beat the eggs. Beat in the sugar. Add the oil, flour, soda, salt, and cinnamon. Add the vanilla and mix well. Stir in the chopped apples and nuts by hand. Pour into a greased and floured 9-inch tube pan. Bake at 350° for 1 hour and 30 minutes.

Remove from the pan and place on a rack to cool. When cool, place on a serving plate and dust well with confectioners' sugar. *Serves 8.*

Playing with Angels

During hiatus when I was seventeen, I was cast in my first stage play. It was being performed in Phoenix, Arizona, at the Sombrero Playhouse, a popular winter season theater for New York and Los Angeles actors. The play was *My Three Angels,* starring Thomas Gomez, Henry Darrow, and Liam Sullivan.

All three stars, who had much theater experience, were very patient with me. Having only worked with a camera and as a single in vaudeville, I had no notion of how to use the stage. I'd sidle right up close to the other actors, and the director became quite exasperated with me. The "buzz" was that I was to be replaced. But, because the rehearsal period was short and the producer felt I could do the part, I was allowed to stay.

Standing backstage on opening night waiting for our entrance, I said to Mr. Gomez, "I think I have to throw up."

He chuckled sweetly and rubbing my back told me to take deep breaths and that it was going to be fine. When the time came to enter, I flew on stage, with my feet never touching the ground. The only memory left of that night is the sound of enthusiastic applause for all of us at the end.

When the curtain came down I was in a daze as people came backstage to offer us congratulations. Flying toward me came the director, who gave me what is now called "an inappropriate kiss," and he said that he and he alone knew that I could do it all along. Yeah, right.

Anyway, I returned the next year and did two more plays and always had a great time. During rehearsals the producer provided a daily lunch for everyone. The crown jewel was a roast beef brisket. No matter what else was offered, there was always this marvelous beef. The aroma of that is emblazoned on my memory. Here are two good methods you might want to try.

BRISKET BRACKER

1 large onion, sliced
1 whole brisket (thick part included)
   Ketchup
   Seasoning salt and pepper
1 large clove of garlic

Place the onion across the bottom of a roasting pan. Season the brisket on both sides and lay it on top of the onion. Cover the brisket lightly with the ketchup and top with finely minced clove of garlic. Cover and roast in a 250° oven for 4 hours to 4 hours and 30 minutes.

Remove the brisket, slice it, replace the slices in the natural juices, and continue roasting uncovered at 250° for 30 minutes for browning. It can be served then or held for later and is great warmed up the next day.

On stage in Phoenix at seventeen with Thomas Gomez, Liam Sullivan, and Henry Darrow in My Three Angels.

ARLENE'S BRISKET

1 piece brisket (thin part only)
   Pepper
1 10¾-ounce can beef bouillon
1 envelope dry onion soup
1 bay leaf

Season the brisket with pepper and then sprinkle with the dry onion soup. Pour the bouillon around the meat (not on top) and add the bay leaf. Place in a covered roaster and cook at 275° for 3 hours to 3 hours and 30 minutes.

Discard the bay leaf. Remove the meat from the pan, slice it, and return to the pan. Cover and reheat or hold.

Tying the Knot

On May 5, 1956, I eloped to Las Vegas with a young sound man on *Father Knows Best,* whom I'd dated only a few times. His name was Richard Smith. To say a hurricane of ill feeling and confusion was created by this immature act is stating it lightly. But the show went on.

When, after a month, we decided marriage wasn't what we thought it would be, we decided a baby would make it better. So, on March 30, 1957, our dear son Brian was born three weeks early, weighing only four pounds and six ounces.

It was a difficult time on the show. Mr. Rodney was furious, Jane Wyatt was disappointed in me, and the wardrobe and camera people had to use their magic to make my changing shape disappear.

This is a perfect spot for the ever-popular pregnant ladies' craving—pickles.

Four months before I gave birth to my son Brian, Billy Gray and I checked out New York City via a helicopter with the Port of New York Authority.

BREAD AND BUTTER PICKLES

3   cucumbers, sliced paper thin with skin
2   medium onions, sliced thin, separated into rings
½   green pepper, cut into thin strips
2   tablespoons salt

In a large pan or bowl place the vegetables in layers and sprinkle with salt. Place a layer of ice cubes on top, then a plate, and then a weight. Let stand for 3 hours and drain.

⅝   cup sugar
⅝   cup vinegar
¼   teaspoon ground mustard
⅛   teaspoon ground turmeric
4   whole cloves

In an enamel or stainless steel pan combine the sugar, vinegar, dry mustard, turmeric, and cloves, and bring to a boil. Add the drained vegetables, and cook for 5 minutes. Place in sterilized jars or in the refrigerator. They will be ready in 5 days.

A Nice Disguise

Jean-Louis prevailed on Mr. Rodney to let me have a nice new outfit that could disguise my shape instead of just letting out the seams on my little-girl dresses. The choice was a gray cashmere

sweater set and a gray wrap skirt, also of cashmere. He knew that wearing soft, beautiful clothes makes one feel better.

Well, Mr. Rodney waited for the right script to come along for me to wear this expensive outfit. And he waited. And he waited some more. Until the big day to wear the outfit finally came. And yes, you got it! I could no longer fit into it.

During this time I was honing my domestic skills, as it hadn't taken a week for me to exhaust my kitchen repertoire. Experimenting and collecting recipes and tips from friends and co-workers got me started on what has been a joy ever since then.

Dick (Richard) made terrific onion rings, and I know you will love these.

I was pregnant when we shot this long, boring courtroom scene, and I fought desperately to stay awake.

ONION RINGS SMITH

Brown onions
Milk
All-purpose flour
Salt and pepper
Shortening

Slice the brown onions, thinly, and separate into rings. Put the rings in a mixing bowl and cover with milk. Cover and refrigerate for at least 30 minutes or longer.

In a resealable plastic bag mix the flour, salt, and pepper. Drain the onions, dredge in the flour mixture, and place on a cookie sheet to rest. In a heavy, 2½-inch deep skillet heat ½ cup or more of solid shortening over medium heat until hot but not smoking. Heat the oven to 200° or warm.

In the hot shortening fry a batch of dredged onion rings to a nice golden color. Remove to another paper towel-lined cookie sheet, salt them to taste, and place the rings in the warming oven. Continue in batches until all are done. These will keep at warm for quite a while.

A Haircut

The timing was perfect, for Brian was due during our six-week hiatus. But the rumor was out that I was not going to return to the show. "Betty" would leave for college and would write letters home, which would be read from time to time in the course of the show.

So hearing that, after filming the last episode and due to give birth in a month, I had my long hair cut off into a cute and more manageable short hairdo. Brian arrived swiftly one Saturday morning, and I was the happiest person alive. But things were not to go so well in the marriage, and Dick, feeling swamped by the responsibility, wanted out.

Soon I got word that they would accept me back on the show, which was all well and good, except that my "ponytail" was gone.

"Don't tell them," the redoubtable Miss Messinger decreed. "Just show up. Then there'll be nothing they can do about it."

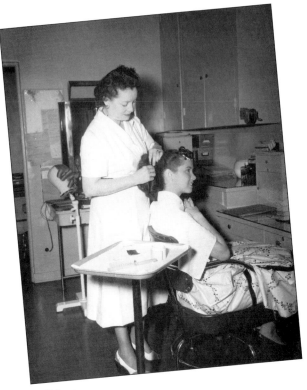

Helen Hunt, head of Columbia's hair department, puts my hair though its paces before a day on the set.

Which brings me to the wonderful Helen Hunt, head of the hairdressing department at Columbia. It fell to her to deal with this problem.

She solved it this way. For a few shows I wore my hair short, while a natural-hair fall was made in the shape of my old ponytail. When the back got long enough to pin in, tortured with a gel and hundreds of pins, the false tail was "nailed" to my scalp. I did the last two years of the show with the false one.

Miss Hunt was an elegant lady who'd been responsible for creating the looks of Rita Hayworth and Kim Novak, as well as doing Jane Wyatt's hair every day.

I'm sure she'd like this recipe.

CHICKEN LIVER MOUSSE

1   pound chicken livers
2   tablespoons minded shallots or green
       onions
2   tablespoons butter
½   cup Madeira or cognac
¼   cup whipping cream
⅛   teaspoon allspice
       Pinch thyme
½   teaspoon salt
⅛   teaspoon pepper
½   cup melted butter
1   tablespoon gelatin
1   10 ¾-ounce can chicken bouillon

In a skillet melt the butter and sauté the livers and onions until the livers are just stiffened but still rosy.

Scrape into a blender jar.

Pour the Madeira or cognac into the sauté pan and boil it down rapidly until it has reduced to 3 tablespoons. Pour into the blender jar with the other ingredients.

Add the cream, allspice, thyme, salt, and pepper. Blend at high speed until the liver is a smooth pâté. Add the melted butter and blend for several seconds more. Force the mixture through a sieve and taste carefully for seasoning. In a separate bowl mix the gelatin and chicken bouillon, and then pour ⅛-inch of the bouillon mixture in a bread pan. Let it jell. Pack in the liver. Chill for one day. If you wish you can mold tarragon leaves or parsley in the jelly.
Serves 6.

Good Girl Gone Bad

Dick and I kept trying and trying to make the marriage work but to no avail. So on the night of my twenty-first birthday we decided to part for good. It was sad. There was no anger. And we remained friends until his death a decade later.

Soon after this, Miss Messinger called with an offer. I was wanted for an independent movie being made at MGM for producer Albert Zugsmith. She sent me the script of *Girls Town* and I turned it down, flat. She indicated that to do so would create ill will, so she, of course, had a plan. She would ask for way too much money, and they would turn her down, thereby making everyone the winner. Her plan backfired. I got the money, but I had to do the movie.

The cast included star Mamie Van Doren, whose baby sister I played. Mel Torme was a tough guy and a young singer named Paul Anka played—what else?—a young singer. Gigi Perreau was a postulant in a nunnery. Besides being Miss Van Doren's blonde sister, I was also the killer.

As the hours at MGM were even longer than at Columbia doing the TV series, Mother moved into the house with me to take care of Brian. This is a quick and easy soup to prepare after a long, hard day.

COLD TOMATO BISQUE

1   cup sour cream
3   cups good quality tomato juice
1½   teaspoons Worcestershire sauce
2   tablespoons fresh lemon juice
1   teaspoon grated lemon peel
1   dash Tabasco sauce
½   cup light cream (half and half)

In a blender combine all of the ingredients and mix well. Chill, and serve.

For a special occasion or dinner party, add a small dollop of sour cream topped with a wee bit of caviar to the center of each serving.

Note: Many, many years later, when Brian owned and was head chef at his Hecker Pass Inn in Gilroy, California, he ran out of the soup du jour late one evening as a large party of local VIPs came in to dine. Of course, they all ordered soup to start. Brian flew to the kitchen, frantically whipped up a double batch of this, and it saved his day. *Serves 4.*

Here I am, a "glamorous" new screen star at twenty-one in my first motion picture role since my child-actress days, as I play Mamie Van Doren's kid sister in Girls Town.

HOODLUM GANG THREATENS GIRL: Mel Torme, seated in the car, is keeping Elinor Donahue in his care in this scene from MGM's Girls Town. *Torme believes that Elinor has been responsible for the death of one of the members of his gang. From left, gang members are John Brennan, with dark glasses; Charles Chaplin, Jr., with arms folded; Jim Mitchum with dark glasses; and Dick Contino, with race helmet and goggles.*

MGM publicity material stated, "Girls Town is a fast-paced, action-packed story of girls who have reached the age of decision—the age where they are physically mature, but emotionally immature—the age of the teens. The large cast is headed by Mamie Van Doren, Mel Torme, Ray Anthony, Maggie Hayes, and introducing Paul Anka. Other important cast members are Elinor Donahue, columnist Sheila Graham, Gigi Perreau and guest stars Cathy Crosby, Jim Mitchum, Dick Contino, Harold Lloyd Jr., Charles Chaplin Jr., Gloria Talbot, and famed singing group The Platters."

Making Music with Jack Jones

After a while, I met, through Lillie Messinger, a young singer who was the son of actress Irene Hervey and singer Alan Jones of "Donkey Serenade" fame. His name was Jack Jones, and, though he was a year younger than I, we began to date.

We enjoyed ice skating and movie going during the time when he was just launching his career by cutting his first best-selling album. A star was born and he is still enjoyed by millions today through his TV, concert, and club appearances.

One of our favorite places to go was Will Wright's Ice Cream parlor for hot fudge sundaes. This Mocha Chocolate Sauce is quick, easy, and dee-licious!

Enjoying a sweet treat with beau Jack Jones.

MOCHA CHOCOLATE SAUCE

6   squares semisweet baking chocolate
½   cup and 1 tablespoon strong black coffee
6   tablespoons sugar
3   tablespoons butter
¼   teaspoon vanilla extract

In a heavy saucepan combine the chocolate and coffee. Over low heat, stir until smooth. Add the sugar and stir to dissolve. Bring to a boil and boil gently for 4 minutes, stirring constantly. Remove from the heat.

Add the butter and vanilla. Stir until the butter is dissolved.

Serve when done or store in the refrigerator for later. It reheats beautifully, but heat it to bubbling before using.

Pour over ice cream of choice. I favor coffee or vanilla, or for a real sweet treat a coffee mocha swirl. Whipped cream (homemade, of course) and nuts and/or cherry are up to you. Indulge yourself.

Jack Jones and I enjoy the ball after the Emmy Awards in 1959.

Up for an Emmy

One of the most exciting times of the *Father Knows Best* years was when I was nominated for an Emmy for best supporting actress in a comedy series in 1959. But I also did another stupid thing. Miss Messinger advised me that I shouldn't drive up in my old 1947 Ford convertible—that I should have a flashier car.

I'd been flirting with a big, huge powder-blue Pontiac, fins and all, that was in a dealership window on the way home from work. I bought the biggy and sold a car I wish I still had. A typical car nut's lament.

I wasn't at all nervous about the prospect of winning or losing an Emmy Award until the afternoon of the big event when a manicurist was putting the last touch on the last finger. That's when both hands started to shake.

Mother accompanied me to the telecast, and Jack Jones was my date for the ball afterward. Mickey Rooney was the presenter of the best supporting category, and among other nominees was Ann B. Davis of *The Bob Cummings Show,* who'd won the year before in that same category. Mickey opened the envelope and stuttered, "Eh, eh, eh," as I began to rise from my seat. He finally got it out, "Eh, eh, Ann B. Davis!"

I confess I was disappointed, but we three went to the ball and had as good a time as possible.

Jack was starring in his first live TV series that was sponsored by a major cola company, so this seems just right here. This is my sister Dede's recipe (Dede is Gwen's nickname in case you think I sneaked in another sister).

COCA-COLA CAKE

1   cup butter or margarine
¼   cup cocoa
1   cup Coca-Cola
2   cups all-purpose flour
2   cups sugar
1   teaspoon soda
½   cup buttermilk
2   eggs, beaten
1   teaspoon vanilla extract
1½   cup miniature marshmallows

In a saucepan combine the the butter, cocoa, and Coca-Cola, and heat to boiling. Remove the pan from the heat. Add the flour, sugar, and soda, and mix gently. Stir in the buttermilk, eggs, vanilla, and marshmallows. Pour into a greased 9 x 13-inch pan. Bake at 350° for 30 to 35 minutes. Frost the cake while warm.

Frosting:
½   cup butter or margarine
¼   cup cocoa
6   tablespoons Coca-Cola
1   cup miniature marshmallows
1   pound confectioners' sugar, sifted
1   teaspoon vanilla extract
1   cup nuts

In a saucepan combine the butter, cocoa, and Coca-Cola and heat to boiling. Remove the pan from the heat. Add the marshmallows, stirring until dissolved. Beat in the sugar and vanilla. Stir in the nuts. Spread over warm cake.
Serves 10 to 12.

Father Retires

In February of 1960, there was a writers' strike in Hollywood, and we were forced to stop work on *Father Knows Best* until it was settled.

However, when the strike was over, we all got word that the show would not resume filming, as Mr. Young refused to continue. He was tired, the scripts were tired, and we three kids had begun to look like three grownups. It was a shock. There were no goodbyes, no party—nothing. I would not, as it happened, see Mr. Young again for almost twenty years.

Though around the corner more work loomed, I would always remember Mr. Young's kindness and sweetness to me when the going was tough.

I recently spent a few quiet moments with him and was able to get the recipe for his most favorite dish, which his wife, Betty, used to make for him.

Robert Young.

STEAK AND KIDNEY PIE

1	pound beef, top round
6	lamb kidneys
2	cups water
1	medium-size bunch carrots, scraped and cut into 1-inch pieces
1	20-ounce can tiny new potatoes, drained
1	10-ounce package frozen lima beans
3	medium Bermuda onions, quartered
2	cups prepared biscuit mix
1	cup milk
¼	small bay leaf
¼	teaspoon thyme
¼	teaspoon sage
	Salt and pepper to taste

Preheat the oven to 450°. Prepare the kidneys by splitting and removing the white membrane. Soak in cold, salted water while cutting the beef into small pieces about the size of half dollars. Sear the kidneys and steak in an iron skillet for about 5 minutes. Add the 2 cups of water and boil for 6 minutes. Put all of the ingredients, except the biscuit mix and milk, in a shallow, buttered casserole and cover with soft dough made from the biscuit mix and milk (do not roll). Bake for 20 minutes.

Note: Now I would blanch those carrots and limas and brown the onions with the meat, but I'm giving it as it was given to me. *Serves 4 to 6.*

Harry and Me

Right after the completion of *Father Knows Best,* I was approached by one of the production executives of Screen Gems, Inc., the TV arm of Columbia Pictures. His name was Harry S. Ackerman, and he'd been keeping an eye on me professionally since coming to the studios from CBS two years before. He asked me to star in a pilot episode for a proposed series called *Calling Miss Peters.*

For this, Helen Hunt turned me into a redhead, but I was no Rita Hayworth and the series didn't sell.

Mr. Ackerman and I spent a good deal of working time together, and the business dinners soon took on the aura of romance. I was divorced, he was in the process of one, and our twenty-four-year age difference seemed like nothing.

He loved to send flowers. One weekend, Mother, Brian, and I came home from shopping to find boxes and boxes of all kinds of flowers on our doorstep. After arranging them in containers, my mother said they made the house smell like a funeral parlor. She was getting nervous, as she sensed a rival in the camp once again.

Harry knew good food and fine wines, and he frequented the best restaurants in Los Angeles, but his real loves were the simplest of dishes. A plain hamburger patty, creamed chipped beef on toast, and the most unusual of all—and the only one he'd make for himself—shrimp and pineapple salad.

SHRIMP AND PINEAPPLE SALAD

1   pound cooked shrimp, medium size,
        cleaned and chilled
1   21-ounce can pineapple chunks
1   rib celery, sliced crosswise
     Salt and pepper to taste
     Mayonnaise

Rinse and drain the shrimp well and cut into large pieces into a medium bowl. Drain the liquid from the pineapple well and add to the shrimp, along with the celery. Add salt and pepper if desired. (Harry liked salt, but no pepper.) Add mayonnaise to taste. Return to the refrigerator (covered, of course) to blend the flavors. Pile onto a lettuce-lined plate and enjoy with a warmed French roll on the side.
Serves 4 to 6.

Harry Ackerman holds Abraham Lincoln's wallet and the famous pen knife. Harry was a lifelong collector of historical memorabilia—mostly Revolutionary War and French and Indian War autographs and such. He made the winning bid on Lincoln's legal portfolio through the Park-Bernet Galleries in New York. Upon receiving the portfolio, he carefully pried the sections apart and saw something glinting in the bottom. He reached in and pulled out the penknife, engraved "A. Lincoln." When his lawyer called Park-Bernet to tell them, they were astounded, as the item had been "lost" for some time. They said it was a clear case of "finders, keepers," to Harry's joy. It was one of his favorite and proudest possessions. He sold the items in the year before his death to the Lincoln Historical Society in Springfield, Illinois.

Moving to Mayberry

During the summer of 1960, I was called for a meeting about a new series to star humorist and actor Andy Griffith. Sheldon Leonard was the executive producer, and Brian and I went to his office one hot afternoon.

By this time Mother and I had come to a serious parting of the ways after a heated argument. We desperately needed more space between us.

Mother retained the house in Woodland Hills, and Brian and I left that very afternoon with no destination in mind, except to get some peace for both of us. I called Mr. Ackerman from a pay phone and he instructed me to drive to a residential hotel in Brentwood, where he would secure rooms for Brian and me for as long as we needed them. I had no money because Mother had always taken care of all my checks and paid the bills. Mr. Ackerman offered to help out with the rent until I could handle things on my own. I felt I owed this wonderful, generous man my life.

Brian was an angelic child. Comfortable with himself, he was bright and funny and affectionate. He and I will always have a special bond.

When Brian grew up, he earned a bachelor of science degree in psychology at Loyola-Marymount; then, marching to his own drum, he became a successful chef in central California. He changed careers in his thirties. He now has his captain's credentials and works for the Monterey Bay Aquarium Research Institute.

He is a marvelous baker and this is one of his favorites, which was also a "Best of Show" winner at the March of Dimes Gourmet Gala at Monterey in 1989.

My son Brian Smith (soon to be Ackerman) at age three shares a hearth-warming time with me on the set of The Andy Griffith Show.

CHOCOLATE-ALMOND TORTE

8 ounces Ghirardelli semisweet choco-
    late
1 ounce strong coffee
1 ounce Chambord (or Amaretto,
    Kalhua, or Grand Marnier)
8 large egg yolks
1 cup butter
1 cup sugar
8 ounces ground almonds
8 large egg whites
    Cream of tartar

In the top of a double boiler over simmering water melt the chocolate with the coffee and Chambord. In a large bowl cream the butter and sugar and add the yolks one at a time. Blend in the almonds, then blend in the chocolate. Whip the egg whites with a pinch of cream of tartar until stiff but not dry, then fold into the chocolate mix.

Preheat the oven to 375°. Pour the mix into a buttered and floured 9-inch spring-form pan. Level with a rubber spatula, making the sides slightly higher than the center. Bake approximately 40 to 50 minutes. Cool, then chill.

Ganache:
1 pound Ghirardelli semisweet choco-
    late
1 ounce dark coffee
3 ounces heavy cream

In the top of a double boiler over simmering water combine the chocolate, coffee, and cream. Pour the ganache over the top of the torte and also brush the ganache on the sides. Garnish the sides with ground toasted almonds.
Serves 6 to 8.

Tranquil Set

I began *The Andy Griffith Show* a few weeks after the meeting with Sheldon Leonard. Brian and I now had an apartment in Westwood and I had found a play school near the studio where I could drop him off on the way to work.

The cast of *The Andy Griffith Show* was wonderful. It was a treat to watch Andy and Don Knotts rehearse as they fine-tuned their characters. Ronny Howard was the finest child actor I'd ever worked with, and Frances Bavier became like a mother to me on the set.

As on most sets, there were always plenty of snacks, and cookies in the afternoon were especially good. See how you like these.

GINGER DROP COOKIES

½ cup shortening
1 cup brown sugar
1 cup molasses
2 teaspoons baking soda in ½ cup boiling water
2 eggs, beaten
1 cup walnut meats
1 cup raisins
   Enough all-purpose flour to make batter drop from spoon (about 1½ to 2 cups)
1 teaspoon ground ginger

1 teaspoon ground cinnamon
   Pinch salt

Preheat the oven to 350°. In a mixing bowl using an electric mixer, cream the shortening. Add in order the sugar, molasses, soda in the boiling water, egg, nuts, and raisins. Combine the remaining ingredients and the add to the mixture. Mix thoroughly. Drop the dough by the spoonful onto a cookie sheet and bake for about 10 to 12 minutes. *Makes 3 to 5 dozen.*

Kidding around on the set while filming "The Beauty Contest" episode of The Andy Griffith Show.

CLOSE-KNIT GROUP—Andy offers some pointers as I stick to my knitting during a break on the Griffith *set.*

Jolly Good Chap

Bernard Fox played memorable cyclist Malcolm Merriweather in three episodes of *The Andy Griffith Show* in years after I was on the show. Bernard's character is one that fans clamor for when he does personal appearances to this day. Though we didn't work together on the show, we have in recent years. Bernard and his wife, Jackie, graciously agreed to share this recipe with you. (You'll hear from Bernard again later, too.)

Bernard Fox as Malcolm Merriweather in the 1965 episode of The Andy Griffith Show *entitled "Malcolm at the Crossroads."*

CORNISH PASTY

The Cornish Pasty was used on The Andy Griffith Show. *Harvey Bullock (the writer) asked me if there was any typical British dish that I could think of, and I suggested the Pasty. It originated with the wives of the Cornish tin miners. They built a little pastry wall across the center, filled one half with the meat and potatoes, and filled the other half with something like strawberry jam, so that you ate your way through the savory to the dessert, which was a line Andy had in the episode ("The Return of Malcolm Merriweather"). I note that the recipe calls for a six-inch ring of pastry, but that seems a bit small to me. Nowadays, it seems to be more convenient in the British pubs to serve them on their sides as it were, but the true Cornish Pasty should be standing up, something rather like an armadillo.—Bernard Fox*

Shortcrust Pasty (Savory):
7	ounces all-purpose flour
	Pinch salt
¼	cup unsalted butter
¼	cup shortening
	Iced water
1	large egg yolk

In a mixing bowl sift the flour and salt. Cut the butter and shortening into small pieces. Use a pastry blender or fork or fingers to blend thoroughly until the mixture looks like fine bread crumbs. In another bowl beat the yolk with 1 tablespoon of iced water. Pour slowly into the flour mixture until the dough begins to bind. Add a little more iced water as needed. Roll the dough into a ball, wrap in grease-proof paper, and then a damp cloth. Store in the refrigerator for approximately 1 hour before using.

Filling:

1½ pounds mincemeat (beef or lamb)
2   large potatoes, diced
2   large onions, diced
2   medium carrots, diced
2   tablespoons, baby green peas
½   teaspoon fresh basil
½   teaspoon fresh tarragon
1   teaspoon fresh parsley, minced
½   teaspoon fresh thyme
     Pinch salt and pepper to taste

1¾ pounds shortcrust pastry (savory)
1   egg, beaten

Preheat the oven to 350°. Mix the beef, vegetables, chopped herbs, and salt and pepper in a large bowl. Mix thoroughly.

Roll the pastry dough into 15 rounds of approximately 6 inches each. Divide the filling and spoon it onto the pastry rounds. Lightly dampen the pastry edges and then fold over so that the ends meet. Crimp the edges of the pastry with a fork to seal. Brush the tops of the pasties with the beaten egg. Bake for 35 to 40 minutes until cooked and the pasties are golden. Enjoy!

Mayberry Musical Note

There is a wonderful episode of *The Andy Griffith Show* called "Christmas Story," which is Mayberry's version of Dickens' *A Christmas Carol.* The episode called for me to sing "Away in the Manger" with Andy accompanying me on guitar. I was quite nervous about making the recording.

Frankly, the idea of singing terrified me. I hadn't sung professionally in years and I just wasn't confident in my voice. Andy Griffith obviously sensed my apprehension and, being a singer himself, he no doubt had had similar feelings of his own from time to time. He suggested that we sit down on the floor of the recording studio just to get comfortable as we rehearsed the song. In fact, we were actually recording—an old ruse used by directors who have a nervous performer.

But the trick worked and the song came off wonderfully. We simply lip-synced the scene to the recording. However, this particular scene was not as routine as most. It called for one sustained shot through the entire length of the song with no cut-aways to closeups. (It's one of the longest sustained shots of the entire series, so I'm told. Because there were no cut-aways, nimble camera movements were needed to follow the action.) It was Bob Sweeney's first episode as director for the series, so I'm sure he felt the pressure more than anyone.

All of the effort paid off. Fans tell me that this scene is one of their favorites of the entire series, and the episode itself has become something of a holiday classic. It was that kind of attention to details in all aspects of its production that kept *The Andy Griffith Show* in television's Top Ten for all of its eight-year prime-time run.

Here's a recipe with a flair of the holiday season that I think you'll like.

CRANBERRY CRUNCH SQUARES

1   **cup quick rolled oats**
¾   **cup brown sugar**
½   **cup sifted all-purpose flour**
½   **cup shredded coconut**
⅓   **cup butter or margarine**
1   **16-ounce can whole cranberry sauce**
1   **tablespoon lemon juice**

Preheat oven to 350°. In a large bowl mix the oats, sugar, flour, and coconut. Mix in the butter until crumbly. Press half of the mixture in a greased 8-inch baking dish. Combine the cranberry sauce and lemon juice and place on the mixture in the pan. Top with the remaining crumb mixture. Pat gently together. Bake for 40 minutes. Serve warm with vanilla ice cream.
Makes 8 or 9 pieces.

"Now, let's see, Ellie. What peculiar kind of Christmas shrub do you reckon this is?"

Mayberry's Rock Star

In addition to his brilliant work with Sid Caesar, Carl Reiner, Mel Brooks, Imogene Coca, and others on *Your Show of Shows,* Howard Morris is perhaps best know by today's rerun fans as untamable rock-thrower Ernest T. Bass, whom Howard played in five episodes of *The Andy Griffith Show* (and in the *Return to Mayberry* movie in 1986).

Howard and I never worked together on the Griffith show, but we have appeared on stage together at several of the Mayberry cast reunion events around the country. Howard has an enormous heart and an incredible, funny mind. He also has a lot of that rascal Ernest T.'s mischief. Exhibit A is his rock candy recipe.

ERNEST T. BASS ROCK CANDY

You can take it for granite that it's almost as sweet as Romeena.
(That's Ernest T.'s Mayberry sweetheart, who was played by Jackie Joseph.)

3   cups sugar
1¼ cups water

First, you find a foil pan that's the size and shape of a window pane at Hogette Winslow's house (about 8 x 8 inches). Then at a point about half as deep as the pan is, you punch 7 or 8 pinholes, about as far apart from each other as your thumb is wide—all the way across one side of the pan, and then you do the same on the opposite side of the pan. Then you take some string and jab it through the holes from one side to other like you were making a possum trap.

Sometimes I like to put masking tape over the outside of the holes to cut down on stuff seeping out, but usually I just put the foil pan inside a larger pan to catch anything that drips out of the holes. Foiled again, I say!

After you've got the pan ready, you dissolve the sugar in the water by cooking it in a pot on high (without stirring) until it's hot enough to make rocks (right at 250°). Next, you pour the syrup into the pan that has the strings. The strings should be covered with almost an inch of syrup. Cover the whole surface with foil.

Now, you'll have time for dancing or for going off into the woods to kill a mockingbird because it might take a week for the rocks to form. (The bestest rocks take time.)

Once the rock crystals have formed, cut the strings from the pan and pry the rocks loose. Wash off the rocks with cold water like a raccoon does and then put them in an oven that's just warm enough for the rocks to dry out and harden up just right.

Now, the rocks are ready for throwin'...I mean, eatin'.

How to get a girl: Make flavored rocks by adding a few drops of your favorite extract. Try peppermint for Christmas or cherry for George Washington's birthday. (See, I really was learning when I got my diploma from my "mother figure"!) And make different colors with food coloring. You'll have the purtiest rocks this side of Old Man Kelsey's Ocean.

HE'S A NUT!—Howard Morris was a scream at a pair of reunion shows commemorating the 35th Anniversary of The Andy Griffith Show *at the North Carolina School of the Arts in Winston-Salem in 1995. A phenomenal twenty-one people associated with the Griffith show appeared on stage that weekend.*
Photograph by Steve Keenan.

A Darling Person

Another wonderful person whose time on *The Andy Griffith Show* followed mine was Margaret Ann Peterson, who played mountain girl Charlene Darling. Maggie, who's married to music virtuoso Gus Mancuso, started out in show business as a singer. We've appeared together at several of the informal Mayberry cast reunion shows in recent years, and Maggie always delights audiences with her singing and personality.

Here's a recipe she shares with us. She thought it might be something that Charlene would make for the Darling family.

SAD CAKE

3   eggs, beaten
1   16-ounce box brown sugar
2   cups Bisquick or baking mix
1   cup chopped pecans
     Whipped cream

In a large bowl mix all of the ingredients except the whipped cream. Pour into a greased iron skillet. Bake at 350° for 30 to 40 minutes.

Serve with whipped cream.
Serves 8 to 10.

Posing in front of a Mayberry squad car replica following a stage show in Birmingham, Alabama, in 1997 are Andy Griffith Show performers (left to right) Keith Thibodeaux (aka Richard Keith), who played Johnny Paul Jason in Mayberry (and who is perhaps best known as Little Ricky on I Love Lucy), Maggie Peterson Mancuso (Charlene Darling), Don Knotts (Barney Fife), Betty Lynn (Thelma Lou), and me.

A publicity shot with Andy Griffith. (A keen fashion eye may have noticed I'm wearing the same blouse I wore for a Father Knows Best publicity shot a few years earlier.)

Changing Stages

By the end of the first season of the Griffith show, I was wrung out—emotionally and physically. Harry Ackerman and I were now at a serious stage in our relationship. Both of us were wanting to marry eventually, but both of us were unable to commit to it. (He too had been through a fairly recent divorce, and he had two wonderful children, Susan and Stephen.)

The rift with my mother was healing somewhat, but it was tentative at best. And I was feeling especially insecure at work—afraid I was not doing a good enough job. That has plagued me all of my adult life.

So, when we finished for that year (with the show ranked fourth for the season in the Nielsen Ratings), I asked my agent to get a release on my three-year contract with the show. In my heart, I hoped that they'd fight to keep me, thereby proving to me that I really was doing the job all right. But release me they did, and that was the end of my time in Mayberry. Once again, I never got to say goodbye. This time, though, it was my own fault!

This soup is to honor not only the South but the likes of little boys everywhere—peanut butter, though with a somewhat sophisticated take on it.

CREAM OF PEANUT SOUP

¼ cup butter
1 medium onion, chopped
2 ribs celery, chopped
3 tablespoons all-purpose flour
2 quarts chicken stock or canned chicken broth
2 cups smooth peanut butter
1¾ cups light cream
   Peanuts, chopped

In a skillet melt the butter and sauté the onion and celery until soft but not brown. Stir in the flour until well blended. Add the chicken stock, stirring constantly, and bring to a boil. Remove from the heat and purée in a food processor or a blender. Add the peanut butter and cream, stirring to blend thoroughly. Return to the low heat and heat until just hot, but do not boil. Serve, garnished with peanuts.

Note: This soup is also good served ice cold.

Makes about 3 quarts.

This 1964 photo shows my stepson Stephen with son Brian and Harry while vacationing in Santa Barbara.

Breathing Room

For once, it seems, a right decision had been made, because I now had time to catch my breath and take a break from work. I had time to enjoy Brian and life and to make some serious plans for our future.

I also had a chance to practice domestic skills without pressure. Brian was an adventurous eater, which was unusual for a child so young. Once in a seafood restaurant at a beach, I perused the menu with a sinking heart because there didn't seem to be anything on it that a small child would enjoy. Harry and I each ordered abalone steak, and I figured Brian would eat my chowder or a salad or something. When the waiter asked, "And what would you like, young man?" Brian piped up, "I'll have the baloney steak." Harry and I looked at each other and shrugged. Did Brian eat it? Every bite.

Abalone is scarce these days and therefore very expensive. And it needs a light touch. Its own flavor and texture is enough.

SAUTÉED ABALONE

1   abalone steak per person (or more, if
     steaks are small)
     Eggs, beaten
     All-purpose flour seasoned with salt
      and pepper
     Butter and wee bit of olive oil
     Fresh parsley, chopped
     Lemon wedges

Pound the steaks to about ¼-inch thickness. Dip the steaks in the egg and dredge in the seasoned flour. In a heavy skillet coated with the butter and oil, sauté the steaks over medium-high heat for 1 minute on one side and 30 seconds on the other. (Any more than that and the steaks will become rubbery.) Sprinkle with the parsley and lemon wedges.

Variation: Instead of using parsley, you can some more butter to the skillet, quickly sauté some slivered almonds, and pour them over the steaks.

A Career
Filled by
Family and
Friends

All Pheasantries Aside

I can't talk about kids being picky eaters without admitting that once I was squeamish too. Harry called to tell me that he was going hunting and would be bringing pheasants to my apartment for me to cook. Checking three cookbooks to find a recipe that sounded easy enough, I was ready when he arrived with this horrible, bleeding package of poor little things.

If we'd been married, I probably would have said something like, "Are you out of your cotton-pickin' mind! Get those things out of here!" But I was the "girlfriend," meek and mild. Somehow we got the birds "dressed," as they say, but the poor dears were peppered with buckshot, which was imbedded in the flesh. Talk about over-kill.

Lesson Number One: Get your pheasants from your friendly butcher.

Harry and I visit at a reception with Seymour Friedman, director of Her First Romance, *the movie I'd done with Margaret O'Brien in 1950.*

WILD PHEASANT

Though my pheasant experience happened nearly forty years ago, I vaguely remember how the birds were done. They were set on a bed of finely chopped vegetables (carrots, celery, onion, parsley, a mire-poix) in a roasting pan. The birds breasts were brushed with butter and seasoning to taste and covered with bacon strips. They were roasted at 400° for about 20 minutes. (When I went to make it again with store-bought pheasants, I couldn't find the recipe. I've hunted and searched and never did find it, so I've never cooked pheasant since.)

Let me give you this side dish that my sister makes that would be wonderful with your own pheasant—or turkey or chicken or....

BAKED CRANBERRY RELISH

1   **pound cranberries**
2¼ **cups sugar**
1   **cup coarsely broken walnuts**
1   **cup orange marmalade**
    Juice of 1 lemon

In a shallow baking pan combine and mix lightly the cranberries and sugar. Cover tightly with foil and bake for 1 hour at 350°.

Spread the walnuts in a separate shallow pan and toast for about 12 minutes, stirring a couple of times. Add the nuts, marmalade, and lemon juice to the cooked cranberries, mix well, and chill.

Makes about 1 quart.

Wedding Belle

I did a bit more work in 1960, the highlight of which was getting all dolled up in a wedding dress. I'd been planning a fancy wedding since childhood, but once again circumstances dictated that it was not to be.

On April 21, 1961, two days after my twenty-fourth birthday, Harry and I flew to Mexico and were married. We spent a few lovely days of honeymoon and then flew to New York City for Harry's business.

I'd never been in New York just for fun before and it was wonderful, though I'm sure his well-placed friends were shocked at my age and lack of sophistication. However, they were all very nice to me and made me feel welcome.

I've mentioned Harry's love of simple foods. One evening an agent friend of his invited us to a pre-theater dinner at Dinty Moore's Steakhouse, famous in New York and known around the country for its canned beef stew. At the restaurant, we were urged by our host to try the stew, but I demurred by telling how, when Mother and I were struggling, that canned stew was all we could afford to eat. Besides (I didn't mention) I didn't like it.

But no, our host laughed, the canned stew was nothing like the real thing, which, we were told, was delicious. So under gentle pressure, I gave in. The dish arrived and sure enough, you couldn't have distinguished it from the canned variety on a bet!

This shepherds pie was told to me by Elizabeth Montgomery, who, though she worked long hours and hard, loved to play in her kitchen, too. This is what she told me.

SHEPHERDS PIE

This is basically something nice you do with leftovers, so what goes in it is pretty much up to you. But this is how it goes:

1   **pound ground beef**
1   **onion, chopped**
1   **clove garlic, minced**
1   **tablespoon good olive oil**

Tomato paste
Canned beef broth
Heinz 57 sauce
Splash Worcestershire sauce

Cooked peas
Cooked carrots
Cooked corn
1   **small can tomatoes, drained and chopped**
Real mashed potatoes
Melted butter

In a large pot combine the beef, onion, garlic, and oil, and cook over medium heat until done and lightly browned. Then add tomato paste, beef broth, Heinz 57 sauce, and Worcestershire sauce to taste. Cook until you have a nice sauce. (Taste as you go and correct.)

Now add the peas, carrots, corn, and tomatoes. Cook on low for a few minutes to blend the flavors. Transfer to a casserole dish and top with mashed potatoes. Brush the top with melted butter. Bake at 350° for 20 to 30 minutes or until bubbly around the edges.

Serves 6.

HERE COMES THE BRIDE—Jay North and I in the "Dennis and the Wedding" episode of Dennis the Menace *in 1960.*

When It Rains, It Pours

We returned to California, bought a small house in Studio City, and settled into domestic life. We had a ready-made family of three children. Susan was fourteen, Stephen was twelve, and Brian was four when we were married. Steve and Sue stayed with us most weekends, and, while there was a difficult adjustment time, it worked out well and we were soon a real family. (Harry also legally adopted Brian as his son.)

One weekend it rained and rained, and then it rained some more. Our house was midway up a hill with nothing across the street but more hill and a dirt access road. The mud began to flow down the road like lava mixing with the heavy rains until the street resembled the Mississippi River. It also began to seep into our kitchen door, which we had to block with towels and bags of kitty litter.

During my Mayberry days.

I had gone to the grocery store on Friday to prepare for the weekend, but since that time we had been stuck home because no cars could get up or down our hill. Most of the food had been eaten by Sunday night.

I don't remember what else we had left (not much, I'm sure), but I had one head of cauliflower, one can of Cheddar cheese soup, and some corn flakes. And so was born a dish called Cauliflower Brian. Why "Brian?" I thought if I named it for him, he'd eat it. He did, and it became an Ackerman classic and a "must" with Thanksgiving dinner.

Harry Ackerman (wearing his CBS "Eye" cufflinks) fools around with Art Linkletter (center) and Red Buttons.

CAULIFLOWER BRIAN

1 head cauliflower, in florets
1 10¾-ounce can Cheddar cheese soup
½ cup half and half
  Melted butter
  Garlic salt
  Pepper
  Paprika
  Dried parsley flakes
  Corn flakes, crumbled

In a saucepan cook the florets in boiling water until barely tender. Drain and refresh with cold water. In a medium bowl combine the soup and half and half. Place the cauliflower in a buttered casserole dish. Pour the sauce over all. In a small saucepan melt the butter. Add the seasonings. Then add the corn flakes to make a crumbly topping. Sprinkle the corn flake mixture over the casserole. Bake at 350° for 20 to 25 minutes or until bubbly and browned.
Serves 4 to 6.

Give Peas a Chance

Shortly after our marriage, we returned to the New York State area for a specific purpose: for me to meet Harry's family and for us to re-trace the trail of his childhood. We flew to New York City and spent a few glorious days before renting a car and driving north to Albany, Harry's birthplace and home to the Flannerys, his and his mother's close relatives.

We had booked reservations in a grim hotel and went to meet the clan in an upstairs room of a popular restaurant of the day. I was nervous, of course, as I always was when meeting new people. But I was not prepared for the Flannerys.

We all got menus and ordered, and then everyone glowered at us—not saying a word. I was most unwelcome and Harry had been a very bad boy indeed, it seemed. They, as a staunch Irish family, were much opposed to these goings on.

But Aunt Catherine, who was the eldest sister in attendance, broke the ice and began to engage us in conversation, and so I became accepted—at least by her and one other sister, Lillian, and Lillian's husband. Harry's mother was a formidable woman, but the rest of the family took the cake.

Harry had flown Mother Anna out to Palm Springs for a holiday before all of this, so we had a chance to meet on neutral turf. She had definite ideas about her food. "I want hot food HOT! And I want cold food COLD!" she stated emphatically and then gave me the following recipe. A wonderful recipe from a wonderful woman.

CREAMED PEAS AND HAM

4   tablespoons butter
4   tablespoons all-purpose flour
2¼ cups warm milk
1   small onion, chopped
    Cooked potatoes, cubed
    Cooked ham, cubed
    Frozen peas, thawed
    White pepper to taste
    Cayenne pepper
    Ground nutmeg

Harry and I enjoy an evening dining out.

In a skillet melt the butter and sauté the onion until a light golden color. Add the flour and cook until it's all combined with the onion-butter mixture. Slowly add the warm milk and blend and cook the mixture until thickened. Add the potatoes, ham, and peas. Season to taste. Keep warm to blend the flavors, and then serve.

Serves 4.

A Tree Blooms in Studio City

In 1962, Peter was born. He looked like a miniature fifty-year-old executive—complete with a receding hairline and a scowl. Some said he looked like a Harry Ackerman "doll." He was a beautiful child and he has grown to be a very handsome man, as was his father.

    Our house had a huge back yard, and we first planted grass for a play space. But it looked naked. So we planted a tree, a jacaranda, the variety that has the beautiful, purple flowers that bloom in May and June. Well, the ones we'd admired around the city must have been there since God created the earth because they are the slowest growing trees in the world! Now, we had this big naked back yard with one pitiful sapling.

    One day I looked out the window, shrieked, and then ran to the phone to call Harry's secretary, Fran Osborne. She became alarmed as I hysterically asked if Harry could come to the phone.

    "What's wrong, dear?!" she asked.

    "We have one bloom on our tree!" I yelled. "It's so pretty!"

She said she'd give him the big news when he came out of a meeting.

We lived in that house for four years, and I'm here to tell you that that tree never bloomed again, nor did it get any bigger.

Fran was a great executive assistant. Harry relied on her to do so much, and she did it all efficiently and with good spirits. She adored Harry, was like an aunt to me, and was a dear, dear friend. She loved vegetables, so I'll put this one in for her, in gratitude for all she did for us.

Harry and Brian (or B-boy, as Harry called him) horsing around in the wide-open pasture that was our back yard.

COUNTRY ZUCCHINI

2   tablespoons good olive oil
1   large onion, coarsely chopped
2   cloves garlic, minced
2   large, ripe tomatoes, peeled, seeded, and chopped
   Salt and pepper to taste
   Fresh or dried basil to taste
   Garlic salt to taste
2   medium to large zucchinis, washed well and sliced

In a skillet heat the olive oil and cook the onions and garlic until tender but not brown. Add the tomatoes and gently cook them until soft. Add the zucchinis and cook until the desired "doneness." You can serve this hot or at room temperature. It's also very good cold with a squeeze of fresh lemon.
Serves 4.

Harry, posing for this photograph taken at the studio, looks like a man preoccupied with whether his jacaranda tree back home has bloomed yet.

Expecting, The Unexpected

While expecting Peter, we discovered to our embarrassment that our Mexican marriage was not recognized in California and a handful of other states. Obviously, this had to be rectified as soon as possible. But I refused to go to a justice of the peace with a big pregnant tummy.

As soon after Peter's birth as I was able to travel, we scooted up the coast to Monterey and Carmel and had a courthouse wedding with the judge's secretary and, yes, the janitor as witnesses. Terry Allen, one of our dearest friends, is from that area. She is a writer, now retired, who has written countless books, including *Doctor in Buckskin* and *Navajos Have Five Fingers*. She doesn't like to cook, but the one thing she'll make is this dessert. It is her signature dish, and she is an angel to let me give it to you.

Harry visiting with our friend Terry Allen.

Standing at the gates of the Carmel Mission after our civil ceremony in Monterey in 1962.

TERRY'S ANGEL DELIGHT

Meringue Base:
6   egg whites
1½ (scant) cups sugar
½   (scant) teaspoon cream of tartar

Preheat the oven to 275°. In a large bowl beat the egg whites and the cream of tartar until very stiff. Add the sugar slowly (1 tablespoon at a time) while beating. Spread on a buttered and floured 10-inch pie plate. (I peak the edges high using a rubber spatula.) Bake for 2 hours to 2 hours and 30 minutes until golden. I sometimes turn off the oven and leave the meringue in until the oven cools.

Filling:
8   egg yolks
1   cup sugar
2   tablespoons grated lemon rind
½   cup lemon juice
1   pint heavy cream

In the top of a double boiler over simmering water combine the egg yolks, sugar, lemon rind, and lemon juice, and cook until thickened. Allow to cool. When the mixture is cold, whip the heavy cream until very firm and then fold it into the mixture. Fill the meringue shell and chill in the refrigerator for 24 hours before serving.
Serves 6 to 8.

Sea Worthy

We had some friends, Dick and Mary Anita Loos Sale, who were writers who lived in Newport Beach. They had a large and comfortable motor yacht, *The Amberjack,* and at least once each summer, we would go with them on an outing. There were lots of laughs and good conversation when we were together.

Mary was a superior cook, both on land and at sea. Cooking on a boat takes a lot of talent and Mary certainly had it. Here is my simplified take on one of her best, her Amberjack stew.

AMBERJACK BISQUE

1   10½-ounce can Anderson's split pea
     soup
1   10½-ounce can Anderson's tomato
     soup
     Curry powder to taste
2   full teaspoons sour cream
     Chopped parsley

In a saucepan heat the soups together. Add
the curry powder and blend in well. Ladle
into warmed bowls and top with sour
cream—giving it a little swirl through, but
leaving a blop. Sprinkle lightly with parsley.
    Mary would put fresh crab meat in
before the end. And on top of the sour
cream, she'd put a bit of fresh caviar.
Serves 2.

Ready for a day of boating in 1960...

...and Harry the seasoned yachtsman at sea in 1962.

Horsing Around

Football and all other sports were very important to Harry, as well as to his son Stephen. Harry had always played ball with Steve and his sister Sue. Before my time in their lives, Harry had owned a horse, and he loved to ride. That reminds me of a funny story that takes place in Palm Springs.

I had learned to ride for that awful movie, *Arkansas Swing,* but I hadn't ridden since then. Harry decided that one day on vacation we would rent horses and take the trails through the desert. He was a seasoned rider and knew what he was doing. He led us up this embankment that rose from the desert floor. Up, up we went as the trail wound around and got narrower and narrower. I got scared-er and scared-er. We eventually came down the other side into a peaceful stretch of desert covered with soft lavender and yellow blooms next to a small river bed that had run off the San Jacinto Mountains. Now *this* was riding!

We were having a fantastic time talking and talking, riding and riding. Harry thought we should probably begin to head back to the stables where we had rented the horses. And so we did, talking and talking,

With Jane Vincent and The Hoosier Hotshots in Arkansas Swing.

until we noticed the light was dimming behind our backs. As soon as the sun dropped behind the high mountains, it was pitch dark. And we were lost.

Most horses will bolt for their stable when turned toward home, but these horses must have been having a good time because we just moseyed along. We guessed where we were by the city lights (God bless 'em) and after passing through a few irate people's back yards, we finally made it to the stables. The horses' owners were glad to see us—and angry, too. But when they saw that the horses were comfortable and when we paid for the extra time, they were fine.

That evening called for a couple of drinks at our favorite watering hole, Don, The Beachcomber, which also had some wonderful Cantonese food. Harry's favorite was Chow Don, an unusual egg dish.

CHOW DON

2 tablespoons vegetable oil
1½ cups frozen (or fresh) peas
½ cup finely diced onion
¼ cup canned water chestnuts, drained and finely chopped

½ teaspoon salt
6 eggs, beaten

In a skillet or wok heat the oil to very hot. Add the peas, onion, and water chestnuts. Stir over high heat for 3 to 5 minutes until the onion is browned. Add the salt and beaten eggs and reduce the heat to medium. Stir the mixture gently until the eggs are set, but not overcooked. Serve over hot steamed or fried rice.
Serves 3 to 4.

Brian on horseback in Santa Barbara in 1963.

Peter's ready to play ball in 1964.

Special Delivery

During 1964, I was asked to return to series television in a show called *Many Happy Returns,* which starred the charming John McGiver. Though I'd kept working in television doing episodes of shows such as *77 Sunset Strip, Dr. Kildare,* and *Have Gun, Will Travel,* my heart was really at home and the work had taken just a few days each time, at most.

The carrot on the stick with *Many Happy Returns* was that I would not be in every episode and therefore could have it all—lots of time with my family and still be in a weekly series.

Wrong again. They would schedule me for a show. I'd make plans for child care. They'd change their minds and cancel that episode, etc. For weeks I tried to find a rhythm in all of this, but it soon became obvious to me that the choice was for family. And to my delight, I found that I was again expecting. That was my out. That, and the show just lasted one season.

This is a super big family or party dish that was given to me by Hessy Heistand, wife of the late radio announcer Bud Heistand. Hessy is a good friend and great party giver and I'm lucky to know her.

HESSY'S CELERY, PEAS, AND MUSHROOM MEDLEY

4   cups Oriental-sliced celery
2   9-ounce packages frozen tiny peas
½   pound mushrooms, sliced
4   tablespoons butter or margarine
1   onion, chopped
1   5-ounce can water chestnuts, drained
    and sliced
1   10¾-ounce can cream of mushroom
    soup
    Salt and white pepper to taste
2   tablespoons butter, melted
1   cup fresh bread crumbs

In a saucepan cover the celery with water, bring to a boil, simmer for 3 minutes, drain, and rinse with cold water. Drain thoroughly.

In a separate saucepan cover the peas with water, bring to a boil, simmer for 3 minutes, drain, and rinse with cold water to stop cooking. Drain thoroughly.

In a skillet melt 4 tablespoons of butter and sauté the onions until limp. Add the mushrooms and sauté them until they release liquid. Add the water chestnuts, soup, and salt and pepper to taste.

Layer the celery and peas alternately with the soup mixture into a buttered 1½- to 2-quart casserole, ending with the soup mixture. Mix the 2 tablespoons butter with the bread crumbs, and sprinkle over top. Bake at 350° for 30 minutes or until bubbly.
Serves 8 to 10.

With John McGiver in a publicity shot for Many Happy Returns. *I played Joan Randall, and John played my father, Walter Burnley, who worked in the complaints department for a store. Mark Goddard played my husband, Bob.*

Getting Into The Swing of Things

As I was soon to have another child in 1965, we went to Palm Springs for a close-to-home get away before his birth in February. The weather was too cool for swimming or sun bathing, and we certainly couldn't ride together. All I wanted to do was rest, read, and sleep, so it was not much fun for Harry.

He decided one afternoon to go to the clubhouse to see if he could get an instructor to teach him to play golf, one of the few sports he had never engaged in. Well, he came back glowing with happiness. It turns out he was a natural for the game. And he was hooked (no pun intended). The golf pro was great and gently instructed him.

Tempered with much encouragement, Harry had found his new sport. He bought the shoes, he bought clubs, he bought a shirt. He was ready. Each day we were there, he would go to his instructor and do it some more. He was getting better and better.

When we returned to town, he had his assistant Fran call the nearest country club to his office at the studio and engage an instructor for him at noon a couple of days a week, so he could continue to improve. Nothing at the first lesson. Nothing at the second. He couldn't address the ball. He couldn't hit the ball. He couldn't do anything right. So that was the end of the great golf saga. The shoes, of course, sat in a closet for years.

Since this story started in Palm Springs, I'm going to give you a fried rice recipe was that was given to me by my friend and neighbor Peggy Ramey. It will go well with the Chow Don or anything else, for that matter.

Harry during his enthusiastic, if brief, foray into the world of golf.

EASY PORK FRIED RICE RAMEY

2   to 3 tablespoons oil
1   cup roast pork, diced
¼   cup scallions in ½-inch sections
4   cups cooked rice, cold
1½ tablespoons soy sauce
½   teaspoon salt
2   eggs, well beaten

In a skillet or wok heat the oil. Add the pork and scallions and stir-fry to coat with oil. Add the rice, soy sauce, and salt. Stir-fry to heat thoroughly. Add the eggs and fold in until well set.

Note: This may seem like egg overkill, but with 2 eggs to 4 cups rice, you'll hardly notice them and they act as a binding ingredient.

Serves 4.

Growing Family on the Move

James was born and it soon became apparent that we had already outgrown our little house. We hated to leave our neighborhood and the friends we made there—including the Volk family on one side and the Bracker family on the other.

Both ladies, Arlene Volk and Phyllis Bracker, were fabulous cooks, but with different styles. One was very gourmet and one was very family. I got this recipe from Arlene one day long ago and have used it innumerable times since.

Two-month-old James takes in the world as big brother Peter and our nanny watch over him.

VOLKSRICE

This was in the days when nobody thought anything about butter. Give 'em more! And according to Robert Young, go ahead and have it.

Lots of butter
2   large onions, chopped
1   pound mushrooms, sliced
2½ cups cooked rice
    Basil to taste
    Salt and pepper to taste

In a large skillet sauté the onions in butter until slightly golden. Add more butter and the sliced mushrooms, cooking through but not browning. Add still more butter and when melted turn off the heat and add the cooked rice and seasonings. Add more butter, if you like (it takes a lot). Transfer to a casserole dish and bake at 350° for 30 minutes.
Serves 6.

Harry poses with William Boyd (Hopalong Cassidy) in this 1956 promotional photo for CBS-TV.

One Busy Man

I've not told you much about Harry's career. After several years of working in radio and advertising, he became an executive producer for CBS-TV in New York. He supervised the development, writing, and casting for all of the network's East Coast programming, including *Studio One* and *Suspense*.

When Harry came to Hollywood as a vice president in charge of programming for CBS-TV, he oversaw series such as *The Jack Benny Show* and *The Burns and Allen Show*. He personally developed the *Gunsmoke* series and organized the development of *Our Miss Brooks* and *I Love Lucy*.

He decided he wanted to produce on his own, and the following season he brought two new shows to TV, *Leave It to Beaver* and *Bachelor Father*. Following that, Harry joined Screen Gems, where *Father Knows Best* was made and where he produced a record twenty series, including *Dennis the Menace, The Donna Reed Show, Hazel, Tightrope, The Farmer's Daughter,* and many others. He was soon to create *The Flying Nun* and co-create *Bewitched*.

Harry was a busy guy, but he always made time for fun and he never discussed business at home. When he left the office—after a very long day, sometimes—he'd leave the work there.

This was one of Harry's very favorite dishes, and I frequently made it at his request. It's really good with a crisp salad and some garlic toast.

Harry at home with son Chris in 1969.

HAMBURGER ACKERMAN

2   tablespoons olive oil
1   pound lean ground beef
1   cup chopped onion
3   cups uncooked noodles

3   cups tomato juice
2   teaspoons Worcestershire sauce
2   teaspoons celery salt (or less, if you
       like; I do)
¼   teaspoon pepper (or more, if you like;
       I do)
1   clove garlic, minced
½   teaspoon dried basil
1   or 2 dashes Tabasco
1   cup sour cream

In a skillet heat the olive oil and brown the meat and onions well. Place the uncooked noodles over the meat. Do not mix in.

In a large bowl combine the tomato juice, Worcestershire sauce, celery salt, pepper, garlic, dried basil, and Tabasco. Add the mixture to the beef.

Cover and simmer for 30 minutes, or until the noodles are tender and the sauce has cooked down. Stir in the sour cream, reheat, and serve.
Serves 6 or, if it's Harry, 2.

Knock on Wood

One of the many people Harry Ackerman worked with in his radio and television career at CBS was Edgar Bergen. He and his beautiful wife, singer and actress Frances Bergen, entertained often and well.

As Mr. Bergen was very proud of his Scandinavian heritage, one of his favorite dishes was Swedish meatballs.

MORE THAN WOOD-BE ENTERTAINERS—Harry Ackerman (center) chats with Edgar Bergen (and Charlie McCarthy).

SWEDISH MEATBALLS

1 pound hamburger
½ pound lean ground pork
1 egg slightly beaten
1 cup milk
¾ cup dry bread crumbs
¼ cup minced onions
1½ teaspoons brown sugar
½ teaspoon white pepper
1½ teaspoons salt
1 teaspoon ground nutmeg
½ teaspoon allspice
   All-purpose flour
¼ cup butter

1 cup cream
¼ cup beer

In a mixing bowl combine the beef, pork, egg, milk, bread crumbs, onion, brown sugar, pepper, salt, nutmeg, and allspice. Form into small balls 1 inch in diameter. Roll the balls in flour. In a skillet melt the butter and brown the meatballs on all sides. Add the cream and beer. Cover and bring to a boil. Reduce the heat and simmer for 15 minutes.
   Serves 6.

Harry gives some last-minute directions to Bob Hope before a Screen Guild Theatre performance.

A Fish Tale

Harry and Desi Arnaz had been great buddies and particularly loved to share their passion for deep-sea fishing. Harry continued fishing until late in life, but in the beginning of our marriage, he wanted to share it with me—especially when the albacore tuna were running.

One time we got out on a boat with Oscar, Harry's fishing guide, and set out to find the tuna. We left in the dark of a cold, damp morning—about 2 or 3 A.M. The excitement was running high among the guys. I curled up in a bunk and went to sleep.

Awakened by shouts and the sound of a running boat, I struggled on deck. It was barely light and the sea was rough. Oscar shoved a pole in my hand and, after a wait, helped me catch that first tuna. He caught it himself, to be honest, with this person wedged between himself and the pole. I hated every moment of it.

Lots of fish were caught that day, and when we returned to the dock, the ever-present photographer (in this case, Dick Ryan) was there to record the triumph.

Harry (far left) enjoys a celebration with Lucille Ball and Desi Arnaz (far right) at the couple's home, along with director Vincente Minnelli.

Now, I may not like fishing for albacore tuna, but I sure like to eat it. This recipe is my friend Annie Byner's favorite sandwich that I've made for her. When having a pre-theater picnic one summer evening, she ate hers and half of mine. And she insists I tell you about it.

TUNA SALAD SANDWICH

2   6-ounce cans tuna, well drained
1   lemon, cut in half
2   ribs celery, scraped and chopped
    (coarse or fine; it's your call)
1   slice red onion or 2 scallions, minced
1   tablespoon fresh dillweed, minced, or
    1 teaspoon dried dill
    Lemon pepper seasoning
    Celery salt to taste
1   or 2 dashes cayenne pepper (optional)
    Good mayonnaise or lemon-herb fla-
    vored mayonnaise dressing
    Lettuce leaf
2   slices bread

Flake the tuna in a bowl. Squeeze the lemon liberally into the tuna (no seeds, please).

Add the celery, onion, seasonings, and as little mayonnaise as possible—just enough to hold it together lightly. Otherwise, it gets sloppy. Put a hint of mayonnaise on one of the two slices of bread (egg bread or whole wheat is my choice), put a lettuce leaf on, put the tuna on that, then the other slice of bread, slice it, and voila!
Makes 1 sandwich.

Frankly, I think the quality of the tuna is the key. Here is where I get mine. They do mail order:
Point Loma Seafoods
2805 Emerson Street
San Diego, CA 92106
Phone: (619) 223-1109

Note the rictus-like smile on my face as I was forced, with Harry laughing hysterically, to hold these poor things by their icky tails.

Pre Game Warm-Up

A beautiful big house, another baby boy (James), a successful husband, and good friends. Even my mother and I were close again as she was now in full "Nana" mode and always ready to come to our aid when we needed her. And with three little boys, that was often.

At this time, Harry had created with Bill Asher the series *Bewitched* to star Bill's wife, Elizabeth Montgomery. Not only did they have a fine working relationship, but the four of us became close friends for many years.

Elizabeth and Bill were football "nuts" and when the Rams played in Los Angeles, we would always go to Scandia on the Sunset Strip for brunch before the game. That had been a tradition for years among many in Hollywood. The food was sensationally good and the atmosphere was warm and club-like, with deep red leather, high-backed swivel chairs around heavy, polished oak tables, and gleaming copper accents on the walls.

There always were drinks to start as the menu was looked at. And Lud, the bartender (who was part owner, but no one knew it), made the most delicious Bloody Marys imaginable. The best thing is they are terrific with no alcohol at all. So I'm going to give the recipe to you as one serving and you can add whatever alcohol you happen to favor.

*Huddling during a game of touch football in Palm Springs are (left to right)
Bill Asher, Larry Hagman, Harry Ackerman, and Elizabeth Montgomery.*

LUD'S BLOODY MARY

3   parts tomato juice
1   part beef bouillon
1   teaspoon Worcestershire sauce
    Dash celery salt
    Dash pepper
    Dash Tabasco
1   small celery stalk as garnish

In a glass over ice pour any alcohol desired (if using), and then add the remaining ingredients. If no alcohol is used, give a nice squeeze of lemon.

This is not only good on its own, but when one is under the weather and food is not desired, it is healthful and filling, but without the alcohol.
Serves 1.

Palm Springs Training

The only sports I've actively engaged in are swimming, bicycle riding, horseback riding, and the old school try at tennis.

I was once encouraged to join in a "touch" football game in Palm Springs after other recruits were sidelined with "previous appointments." Team sports with flying balls are not my thing, but I decided to give it a try. I mean, they were all laughing and having fun, right?

So I went into the huddle. You go here. I'll go there. Blah-blah-blah. And we began. I swear I went where I was supposed to go. The first thing I see is my husband with a maniacal look on his face and coming at me like a freight train. He hit me right in the Adam's apple. That was the end of my football career.

For many years in Palm Springs, there was a restaurant called The Dolls House, where they served a potato dish called, simply, Those Potatoes. I got this recipe from noted Beverly Hills hair stylist Neil Sloan for his take on Those Potatoes.

THOSE POTATOES

2   parts butter, 1 part olive oil
3   baking potatoes, peeled and thinly
      sliced
4   slices bacon, cubed
1   onion, diced

In a skillet heat the butter and olive oil on medium high heat. Add the potatoes and cook, stirring until nearly transparent. Throw in the bacon and cook until it begins to turn golden. Don't rush it. Next put in the onion and cook until golden brown and crispy.
Serves 2.

Here I am (far left) playing in my one and only game of football in Palm Springs. Lined up on the ferocious defense are Larry Hagman, Bill Asher, Harry "The Hangman" Ackerman, and Elizabeth Montgomery.

Taking Stock

When James was five months old, I was asked to appear in a summer stock production of Muriel Resnick's delightful comedy, *Any Wednesday,* in Sullivan, Illinois. I was hesitant to go, but Harry really wanted me to do it and so, enlisting Mother's help, I left home for three weeks.

The deal was good, and part of any negotiation is which hotel the actor is put up in during the run of the play. My agent called to say that I would be staying at the Palmer House in Sullivan. He and I were impressed because the Palmer House in Chicago was a very nice place indeed.

After a long day of travel, I arrived in Sullivan to be met by the producer and owner of the theater, Guy Little. He indicated that he'd like to take me to dinner to discuss the play, but that first he'd take me to the Palmer House to drop off my bags and freshen up.

We drove into town. We drove through town. We then turned left down a side street and pulled up in front of a cute, well-kept home.

"Well, here it is," Guy said. "The Palmer house. The Palmers are lovely people, and I know you'll be comfortable there.

Since I was not allowed kitchen privileges, I had to find a place in town for all meals. One—and I think there was only one at that time—breakfast and lunch spot served terrific oatmeal.

Here is a new one you might like.

At the breakfast table in the summer stock production of Any Wednesday.

ORCHARD OATMEAL

1   cup quick-cooking Irish oatmeal
2   cups apple cider or juice
1   apple, peeled, seeded, and diced
¼   cup raisins (optional)
½   teaspoon ground cinnamon (or to
     taste)
¼   teaspoon salt (may omit)
¼   cup walnut meats, broken into small
     pieces

In a medium saucepan combine all of the ingredients except the walnuts and cook according to the package instructions for plain oatmeal. Before putting the cover on the saucepan, stir in the walnuts and let it stand for 1 minute. Serve with brown sugar and milk.
Serves 2 to 3.

Things are looking up for me as Ellen (a role originated by Sandy Dennis on Broadway) in Any Wednesday.

Just Right for the Occasion

When James was two years old, I began to work in television a bit again. Harry had a series on NBC-TV called *Occasional Wife,* starring Broadway musical-comedy star Michael "Mickey" Callan and Patricia Harty. It was a bright and energetic show that was on for too short a time. I had a guest role in one episode.

Mickey Callan shared with me his favorite things to eat. He likes arugula salad and a fish starting with an "R." On reflection, my guess is that the fish is orange roughy, because I share that enthusiasm.

Here are a roughy recipe of mine and a salad dressing from son James's wife, Martha, that I have enjoyed at their homes many times.

Posing with Mickey Callan and Pat Harty in a publicity photo from my episode ("Oil Be Seeing You") of Occasional Wife *in 1967.*

MEDITERRANEAN ROUGHY

Sauce:

    Olive oil
1   to 2 cloves garlic, chopped
1   red bell pepper, seeded and sliced
1   green bell pepper, seeded and sliced
1   16-ounce can tomato pieces in sauce
½   cup fresh flat leaf parsley, chopped
2   or 3 leaves fresh basil, chopped
6   Greek olives, pitted and chopped

1   to 2 pounds orange roughy (or 4 pieces)
    Olive oil
    Lemon pepper
    Black pepper
    Paprika

6   stuffed green olives, cut in half crosswise
1   tablespoon (to taste) capers, drained

For the sauce, in a sauté pan heat the oil to medium and put in the garlic for a minute, being careful not to brown. Add the peppers and cook. Add the tomatoes, parsley, and basil. Add the olives and capers and heat through.

Coat the roughy on both sides with the olive oil and seasonings and place in a pre-heated, very hot broil pan. Broil on one side until done. Put each serving on a plate and top with the sauce. Garnish with lemon wedges.
Serves 4.

SALAD DRESSING FOR ARUGULA

2   cloves garlic, finely chopped
1   tablespoon lemon juice
3   tablespoons balsamic or red wine vinegar
1   teaspoon honey mustard or Dijon mustard
    Dash Tabasco
    Salt and pepper to taste
1   cup olive oil

In a food processor combine all of the ingredients, except the olive oil. Then add the olive oil in a slow, steady stream and process until well combined.

Note: For a great bottle to use for salad dressing, buy a single bottle of Grolsh beer with the airtight lid. Dressing lasts a lot longer in this bottle than most others.

Changing at Warp Speed

One day in 1967 I got a call at home from Gene Roddenberry (not to be confused with Gene Rodney of *Father Knows Best*). He wanted to know if I'd be interested in playing an unusual two-character part in his news series, *Star Trek*. I said that I'd talk it over with Harry and get back to him.

Obviously, I said yes, and was it ever a good decision. The episode was called "Metamorphosis" and not only was it fun to play two parts, but it was really fun sitting in make-up in the morning next to Leonard Nimoy as he had his Spock ears put on.

I was on the show a long time, which was both good and bad. I was supposed to be finished in three or four days, but something happened in the film lab, and the landing craft scene had to be completely reshot. By the time the company heard this news, the huge set had already been torn down and had to be rebuilt. Since the soundstage was already being used for other scenes, the crew had to wait a week or more before they could begin to re-build the other set.

In the meantime, I came down with a terrible case of the flu, and when I returned, my little green outfit was just hanging on me from all of the weight I had lost. The

BONES OF ATTENTION—I seem to have the interest of Dr. "Bones" McCoy (DeForest Kelley), but Mr. Spock is otherwise occupied in this publicity shot for the "Metamorphosis" episode of Star Trek.

inventive costumer came up with the long scarf that was draped over my head and across my bony chest. It turned out to be a happy accident, as it was decided to use that scarf in a scene that remained Harry's favorite of all time.

Jerry Finnerman set up the shot using the scarf, which was transparent, like a scrim, in front of the camera. I held it and slowly lowered it as the scene began. Mr. Finnerman had lit it in such a way that I was I was told by him not to move one inch in any direction, but to remain completely still. I was sure I couldn't do it, as I had a long line to deliver, but he said, "Don't move your head; just use your eyes." How right he was. It turned out to be very effective and a nice scene.

And as for happy accidents, some years ago, a neighbor decided to grow some tomatoes. A beautiful, warm summer followed a perfect spring, and Len Felber was now giving everyone he knew these juicy ripe tomatoes. This recipe was born from that bounty.

BAKED TOMATOES

5   medium-sized ripe tomatoes, peeled and sliced
1   cup crumbs, crumbled from packaged onion and garlic croutons
1   scant teaspoon sugar
    Freshly ground pepper to taste
3   tablespoons melted butter

In a small bowl combine the crumbs, sugar, pepper, and melted butter. In a buttered casserole layer the sliced tomatoes and crumb mixture, ending with crumbs. Bake at 350° for 25 to 30 minutes until golden and bubbly.

Let rest for 5 minutes before serving. It's out of this world!
Serves 4.

I'm telling Glenn Corbett that he must leave, but that I will die if I am removed from the planet in our episode of Star Trek.

Fright Night

Halloween was always a big deal at our house. Sometimes we'd have a party and sometimes we'd just gather with the family. But it was always fun.

The best part, besides the costumes and joining all of the other families in the neighborhood tromping through the streets, was my mother's popcorn balls. Unfortunately, she kept the recipe in her head and when she passed away at age ninety-seven, it went with her. That's just as well because she had the magic touch—so much so that I never wanted to try.

Each year, word spread around the Sherman Oaks/Encino area about these popcorn balls at this particular house. When she stopped making them in her eighties, our Halloween "business" dropped off considerably. The only popcorn balls that I've ever tasted that are anywhere near as good as hers are at Topsy's Candy and Popcorn in Kansas City, Missouri. Try their vanilla ones. Their phone number is 1-800-722-1930, but don't tell them I told you.

One silly thing I liked to do was get those little plastic bugs and spiders, wash them really well, place one in the center of individual gelatin molds, and then carefully pour prepared orange gelatin on top. When the gelatin is firm, unmold the gelatin, place it on a lettuce leaf, and serve. It's a scream!

The following are a couple of recipes that youngsters ten to twelve might like to help with for a Halloween supper.

CORN DOGS

1 cup all-purpose flour
2 tablespoons sugar
1 teaspoon salt
1½ teaspoons baking powder
⅔ cup cornmeal
2 tablespoons shortening
1 egg, slightly beaten
¾ cup milk
1 pound frankfurters
 Ketchup
 Mustard

In a mixing bowl sift the flour, sugar, salt, and baking powder. Stir in the cornmeal.

Cut in the shortening until the mixture resembles coarse meal. Mix together the egg and milk and then stir into the cornmeal mixture until blended. Insert a wooden skewer into the end of each frank. Coat evenly with the batter. Fry in deep fat heated to 375° until brown. Drain on paper towels and serve with ketchup and mustard.

 Note: Make sure that the little ones are aware of and careful with the wooden skewers when eating.
Makes 10.

PUMPKIN CAKE

2 large eggs
1 cup sugar
⅓ cup salad oil
1 cup canned pumpkin
1¼ teaspoons salt
¾ teaspoon baking soda
¾ teaspoon ground allspice
¾ teaspoon ground cinnamon

Preheat the oven to 350°. In a large bowl beat the eggs, sugar, oil, and pumpkin until thoroughly blended. Set aside. In a separate bowl combine the flour, salt, baking soda, allspice, and cinnamon. Add to the pumpkin mixture and stir just until blended.

Pour the batter into a greased 8-inch cake pan. Bake for 35 to 40 minutes.

Cool for 5 minutes, then remove the cake to a cake plate. When the cake is completely cooled, frost with icing.

Icing:
½ cup butter, softened
1 cup confectioners' sugar, sifted
½ teaspoon vanilla extract, or ¼ teaspoon lemon extract
1 tablespoon milk

In a medium bowl beat all of the ingredient together until blended and fluffy.

Use your imagination after frosting to make a good Halloween presentation. Have fun!
Serves 10.

James (age three) and Peter (age six) check out their bountiful harvest from Halloween in 1967.

My mother, the Popcorn Queen, poolside in 1967.

Tender Time

A cloud was on the horizon. At two years old, James was diagnosed with pediatric epilepsy, and, as not as much was known about it then as now, I was not aware in the beginning how serious it could be. He was put on medication and we were told to administer it until the seizures stopped. But how do you know? We didn't. And in a year, they began again. By then, the old prescription medication was ineffective.

Also, I found to my delight that I was pregnant again. And unlike my other pregnancies, this time I craved meat. And garlic. Lots of garlic. It's said that cravings are caused by something the baby needs, and garlic is purported to be good for the blood, and it happened that I was very run down.

Peter and I help James (right) celebrate his second birthday at a party in 1965.

This leg of lamb really filled the bill for me and others because of the shape of it. Some parts are more rare than others and some parts are only a wee bit pink. Everyone's happy.

BUTTERFLIED LEG OF LAMB

Marinade:
¾   cup vegetable oil
¼   cup red wine vinegar
½   cup chopped onion
2   to 3 cloves garlic, bruised
2   teaspoons salt (I use less)
½   teaspoon dried oregano, crushed
½   teaspoon dried basil, crushed
1   bay leaf, crushed
¼   teaspoon freshly ground pepper

1   leg of lamb (approximately 5 pounds; have butcher bone, butterfly, and flatten it a bit)

In doubled plastic bags (one inside the other for strength) combine the marinade ingredients. Place the bags in a large bowl and add the leg of lamb. Seal tightly. Turn to coat the lamb well and refrigerate for 24 to 48 hours, turning now and then to marinate the meat.

Broil over medium coals (or in an oven broiler as the stove directs), turning the meat 2 or 3 times and also basting occasionally while cooking for 30 to 45 minutes (use your judgment). The finished meat should be crusty on the outside and pink to rare on the inside.

Harry Ackerman and Elizabeth Montgomery proudly display the awards they were presented by Radio and Television Daily *magazine in 1964.*

A Taste of Merry Old England

Elizabeth (Montgomery) Asher and I were running neck and neck in the baby race. She'd have a boy and I'd have a boy. Poor Harry was getting hit by both barrels—at home and at work. So he did the only sensible thing. He wrote a project to be filmed in England. He was no dummy. He got as far away as he could and escaped the nesting process this once.

His other shows were doing very well and were able to stand on their own. And *Bewitched* was racking up honors right and left.

His London-based show was called *The Ugliest Girl in Town* and was definitely before its time. It was in the same vein as *Tootsie,* a big hit for Dustin Hoffman years later. The stars were delightful and the production values were good, but the series failed. However, it had served a purpose. Harry was only home for a few days every now and then for the better part of a year.

This is a recipe I got from Elizabeth, who loved to entertain and always put out a munificent spread. She came from British stock and this seems the right place for it.

POTTED SHRIMP

1	pound bay shrimp, cooked and brought to room temperature
½	pound butter, softened to room temperature
1	tablespoon lemon juice
½	teaspoon ground mace
	Pinch cayenne pepper
	Pinch fresh black pepper
	Pinch salt
	Fresh toast triangles

Chop half of the shrimp and reserve. Place the remainder of the shrimp in a blender. Add half of the butter and the lemon juice. Purée to a paste. Mix the reserved shrimp into the paste and add the seasonings. Press the mixture into a 3-cup mold or ramekin. Melt the remaining butter and pour into the mold. Refrigerate until the butter is firm. Present in the mold or out and serve with toast triangles that are hot and buttered. *Serves 6 to 8.*

Elizabeth and Bill Asher and Harry and me at one of the many ceremonial banquets that came with the territory.

Dr. Bombay, Come Right Away

One of Harry's, Bill's, and Elizabeth's favorite characters in *Bewitched* was Dr. Bombay, played by Bernard Fox. Audiences took him to their hearts in this role, just as they had his Malcolm Merriweather character on *The Andy Griffith Show.*

The whole world recognized his familiar face in the all-time biggest box-office film, *Titanic,* in which he plays Col. Archibald Gracie. This great man has had a tremendous career. I know you'll like Bernard's "veddy British" curry.

Bernard Fox as Dr. Bombay, always a welcome guest on Bewitched.

DR. BOMBAY'S SHRIMP CURRY

This curry is delicious. We use fresh herbs and put them inside two pieces of celery. We wrap the celery in cheese cloth and then, when the cooking is finished, we fish out the celery with the herbs nicely enclosed inside.—Bernard Fox.

2	pounds fresh boiled shrimp
4	ounces butter
1	clove garlic, crushed
1	large onion, finely chopped
3	ribs celery, chopped
1	green pepper, seeded and chopped
1	carrot, chopped
2	tomatoes, peeled and chopped
1	tablespoon chopped parsley
1	bay leaf, crumbled
	Pinch thyme
	Pinch marjoram
	Pinch dried mint
2	cloves
1/4	teaspoon basil
2	tablespoons all-purpose flour

2	tablespoon curry powder
1/2	teaspoon salt
1/2	teaspoon pepper
1/4	teaspoon cayenne pepper
2	cups consommé
1	cup dry white wine
	Boiled rice
	Chutney

In a large saucepan melt the butter over medium heat. Add the garlic, onion, celery, green pepper, carrot tomatoes, parsley, bay leaf, thyme, marjoram, mint cloves, and basil, and sauté until soft. In a small bowl combine the flour, curry powder, salt, pepper, and cayenne pepper. When the vegetables are soft, sprinkle the curry mixture over the contents of the saucepan. Stir well and cook for about 5 minutes. Slowly add the consommé. When the texture begins to thicken, add the wine. Cook over low heat for about 30 minutes.

If you like, you can strain the sauce from the mixture. Add the shrimp and cook for about 10 minutes, being careful not to let the shrimp overcook. Or you can add the shrimp to the sauce, complete with all of the vegetables. Serve over a bed of fluffy rice. (I prefer a curried rice for this dish.)
Serves 4 to 6.

Marvelous Bernard Fox performs on stage during a Mayberry show that he and I and nine other Andy Griffith Show *veterans did during OxfordFest in Oxford, Alabama, in 1995.*
Photo by Karen Leonard.

Intensive Caring

As the time of the baby's birth neared, Harry had his young assistant Norman Kurland (now a successful literary agent), standing by. Norm was absolutely terrified that he would have to rush over and take me to the hospital. But luck was on our side. Harry had just returned, once again, from England.

We drove to the hospital and waited through a much longer than usual labor. When he came to see me in the delivery room, Harry never let on that there was a concern. But this boy did not look as well as the others had.

Harry drove home after one A.M. and sat up with Mother talking and drinking coffee because he feared the worst. At three A.M., the phone rang with the news that I was hemorrhaging and the baby's lungs were immature and would not stay inflated.

Harry rushed back to find that I had been stabilized in the meantime, and to see our pretty little fellow for what he feared would be the last time. The hospital staff kept trying their best. When our pediatrician was called for a consultation, he strongly recommended that the baby be moved by ambulance to a hospital with the newest technology for caring for infants in peril.

A couchful of Ackermans. Joining Harry and me for this 1968 portrait are sons (left to right) Christopher, Peter, James, and Brian. Oh, and the four-legged Ackerman is Bart, a mixed breed.

They brought him to me, not telling me how serious his condition was. Of course, like all new mothers, I unwrapped him. I thought, "Gee, he's a dark baby." But he was so pretty—lots of black hair and little red lips like a rosebud. We named him Christopher Asher.

At six A.M. he was taken to Good Samaritan Hospital in Hollywood, where he stayed for several weeks and then gratefully was allowed to come home to a very welcoming family.

When I came home from the hospital, all I wanted to eat was chocolate. The name of this cake from one of Harry's associates does not mean the cake is awful. It means it's awful for you, but sooo good!

JOHN THORNE'S TRULY AWFUL CHOCOLATE CAKE

1   3-ounce package instant chocolate pudding

1   18¼-ounce box Duncan Hines devil's food cake mix

1   12-ounce package semisweet chocolate chips

2   eggs

1¾ cups sour cream

Preheat the oven to 350°. In a large bowl mix together all of the ingredients and pour into a buttered and floured bundt pan. Bake for 50 to 55 minutes or until the cake springs back when lightly pressed. (A cake tester will still emerge sticky.)
Serves 10.

Christopher, Harry, and I are all enjoying a rest in this 1968 photograph. (Well, O.K., one of us is resting a little more than the other two.)

Family Times

A happy summer was had by all and soon Elizabeth Asher had her next baby. A girl! At last someone had a girl. She was a beautiful child and they named her Rebecca. Often there was a gathering of the clans with Willie, Robert, and Rebecca Asher at the mercy of the wild Ackerman boys. Mine were a handful, especially James.

James, now under the care of a good neurologist, seemed to be doing better, but we had to watch him carefully all the time. Chris was now completely healthy, and Peter and Brian grew and thrived.

Every Sunday afternoon, if we weren't at the Ashers', would be Barbecue Day, with Harry presiding over the covered cooker. For Harry, it wasn't a real barbecue without huge flames rising up. I'm talking huge! Brian, upon seeing one of these flare-ups, observed, "Ahh, burnt offerings!"

My stepson Stephen and his wife, casting agent Francine Selkirk, have provided me with this easy turkey recipe.

Having a ball at our pool with Brian and James in 1968.

THANKSGIVING BARBECUED TURKEY

1   whole turkey (select any size turkey that will fit your barbecue grill—preferably a Weber; take out the giblets and use for gravy)
     Olive oil
     Salt and pepper

Rinse the turkey thoroughly with cold water. Drain and dry. Rub the bird with oil and salt and pepper. (Sometimes I rub the skin with an herb mixture of 1 teaspoon each of thyme, rosemary, parsley, sage, and basil, plus oil.) You can also put butter under the skin. Try any additions you like.

Secure the legs and tail with metal skewers. Put the turkey in an oiled roast holder and position it on the grill. Directly over the drip pan (for the indirect cooking method) to catch the drippings. Cook the turkey for 11 minutes per pound if not stuffed (13 minutes per pound, if stuffed). The cooked temperature should be 185°.

This method of cooking calls for the placement of the drip pan in the bottom of the grill kettle—directly beneath the turkey. Place about 20 briquettes on either side of the drip pan. You'll need to add more briquettes after about an hour in order to keep the heat even.

Note: During Thanksgiving, we stuff the turkey with cornbread-apple dressing. It's delicious. During the rest of the year, we don't stuff it, and it's just as good.
Allow 1 pound of turkey per person.

It's Beginning to Taste a Lot Like Christmas

James, Peter, Brian, and Chris on Christmas Day 1968.

Christmas was a particularly big deal at our house. Lots of toys, lots of noise, and lots of food.

Harry was an overly generous and expansive man, and he bought many too many gifts for all of us. And it is only in recent years that I've come to appreciate the true meaning of Christmas. But back then, bigger was better and "more" was the operative word.

We always had the traditional turkey dinner. With Harry, it was a must. Thanksgiving was the dress rehearsal for the Big One. Over the years, the Christmas dinner evolved very slowly, if at all, because change was looked upon with dismay. But the candied yams have gone through change, and here is the way I make them now.

CANDIED YAMS

6   medium yams or sweet potatoes
¾   cup good maple syrup
2   tablespoons or more butter
¼   cup water
     Salt and pepper
     Ground cinnamon

Preheat the oven to 325°. In a large pot boil the yams until tender. Peel and slice cross-wise and place in a shallow, buttered baking dish—overlapping the yams to create a nice presentation. Cover with the maple syrup. Dot with butter. Add the water and then salt, pepper, and cinnamon to taste. Bake for 35 to 45 minutes, basting occasionally until cooked down and browning.
Serves 6.

Knock Out Punch

Here's a holiday story I've got to share with you. Lew Bracker gave us this easy and fantastically delicious eggnog recipe. So, one New Year's Eve I made it for a party. The nice thing about it is that it will keep in the refrigerator for at least another day, and we did so with the leftovers of it.

On New Year's Day, the father of Chris's best friend came over to our house to watch part of the Rose Bowl game with Harry. We offered him some eggnog. He sipped slowly, and after a while, Harry offered him a refill. Later, Harry made himself a cocktail and gave the fellow yet another refill (at his request). About that time, the man's wife showed up wanting to know where he was. He smiled at her and was contrite, and bade us goodbye. The only problem was that he could not get up. He was "hammered" to the chair. So a word to the wise is sufficient.

The Ackerman family's all here for the 1972 Christmas episode of Temperatures Rising, *a medical sitcom starring Cleavon Little (seen here as Santa), which was produced and directed by Bill Asher.*

LEW'S EGGNOG

1	dozen eggs
½	cup sugar
1	quart milk
¼	teaspoon vanilla extract
1	pint rum
⅔	bottle bourbon
	Ground nutmeg
3	or 4 quarts vanilla ice cream

Separate the eggs. Beat the whites until stiff and set aside. Beat the yolks while adding sugar gradually until thick and "lemony" looking. Put the mixture in a punch bowl and add the milk (blending well), vanilla, rum, and bourbon. Fold in the reserved egg whites. Refrigerate.

About 2 hours before serving, remove the mixture from the refrigerator and add 2 whole quarts of vanilla ice cream. Sprinkle with nutmeg. After about an hour, check the mixture for consistency and coldness. Add another quart (or more) of ice cream. This will stay cold, thick, and creamy for hours. And if any is left after the party, put it in containers for the next day. It is still great! *Makes about 1½ gallons.*

Well, Aisle Be Darned

After Chris had come home from the hospital and life had settled down a bit, Harry executive-produced a movie of the week for ABC-TV starring Eve Arden and others called *In Name Only.*

It was about a bridal consultant who mistakenly hires an actor, not a clergyman, to perform three weddings in a row and doesn't find out about her mistake until a year later. She then has to track down the couples and give them the news that they're not really married at all. I was Bill Dailey's bride. He had co-starred in *I Dream of Jeannie* and of course went on to *The Bob Newhart Show* and other fine work.

I was so tired while filming this movie that I thought I'd drop. The set photographer used a long lens to capture me in an unguarded moment. It turned out to be Harry's favorite photograph of me.

Since there were lots of actors and personalities in this production (call us hams?), let's make one of Harry's other "most favorite" dishes.

GLAZED HAM LOAF

1½ pounds ground smoked ham
1½ pounds ground fresh pork
1 cup finely crushed saltine crackers
1 cup milk
2 eggs
1 cup brown sugar
½ teaspoon dry mustard
½ cup cider vinegar, diluted slightly
    with water

Blend the ground meats together (or have a butcher do so for you). Combine the meat with the cracker crumbs and moisten with the milk and eggs. Shape into a loaf in an oval or rectangular baking pan (an oven-to-table type is nice). In a bowl make a sauce of the brown sugar, mustard, and vinegar. Pour over the loaf. Bake at 350° for 1 hour to 1 hour and 30 minutes, basting frequently with the brown sugar sauce in the pan. *Serves 6.*

Bill Daily and I just thought we'd tied the knot in 1969's In Name Only.

This was Harry's favorite photograph of me, which was taken on the set of In Name Only.

Smokey chili chef Mike Henry.

It's A Jungle Out There

Each year in television, many pilots are made, but few are ever picked up for a weekly series. One of the cutest pilots that Harry ever made was *Taygar of the Jungle.* It was a half-hour spoof of the Tarzan movies and it was hilarious—only not hilarious enough for the networks.

It starred former football player Mike Henry, who did a masterful job in what was to him a new medium. He was a natural and went on to do many, many movies and TV shows (including playing Jackie Gleason's son/dim deputy sheriff in the *Smokey and the Bandit* movies). The many fans of ABC-TV's *General Hospital* know him as Rudolpho.

When Mike was linebacker for the Los Angeles Rams, I asked him what he ate to keep in such fine shape. With a twinkle in his eye and a mischievous grin, he confessed, "Steak...and cookies!"

This is Mike's chili recipe and it can be a hot one!

MIKE'S CHILI

1   pound ground beef
1   teaspoon butter
1   large onion, cut up
1   16-ounce can kidney beans
1   teaspoon chili powder
     Tabasco sauce to taste
1   16-ounce can tomato sauce

In a big pot brown the ground beef in the butter. Stir in the onion. Add the remaining ingredients (including as much Tabasco as you like). Cook slowly until done.
Serves 4 to 6.

I Like Cake

One June, Chris and Rebecca Asher celebrated their birthdays together at a small park in Beverly Hills near the Asher home. When we picked her up, Rebecca wasn't too sure about the whole thing because I had never taken her anywhere alone before. But she soon was smiling, and this photograph is a treasure to me.

How about this cake for a birthday party picnic? It was also one of President Eisenhower's favorite cakes.

Rebecca Asher and Chris celebrating their birthdays.

DEVIL'S FOOD CAKE

2½ cups all-purpose flour
1   teaspoon baking soda
1   teaspoon (rounded) baking powder
¼   teaspoon salt
½   cup butter
2   cups sugar
3   eggs, separated
1   teaspoon vanilla extract
⅔   cup cocoa dissolved in ½ cup boiling
    water
1   cup sour milk (or buttermilk)

Preheat the oven to 375°. Sift the flour, soda, baking powder, and salt. In a mixing bowl, cream the butter and slowly beat in the sugar. Add the egg yolks and the vanilla. Add the cocoa. Add the flour mixture alternately with the milk. Fold in the stiffly beaten egg whites. Pour the batter into 2 greased layer cake tins. Bake for 25 minutes.

7-Minute Frosting:
2   egg whites, unbeaten
1½ cups sugar, finely sifted
5   tablespoons cold water
½   teaspoon cream of tartar or 2 table-
    spoons light corn syrup
1   teaspoon vanilla extract

In the top of a double boiler combine the frosting ingredients. Stir until the sugar dissolves. Then place over briskly boiling water. Beat with an egg beater for 6 to 10 minutes until stiff enough to stand in peaks. Add the vanilla and beat until thick enough to spread. During cooling, keep the sides of the double boiler cleaned with a spatula. With an electric beater, the process may take as little as 4 minutes.
Serves 8 to 10.

Drop By But Please Don't Drip

There were lots of "dress up" parties in the '60s and '70s. People entertained a great deal, and one the most popular social gatherings was the cocktail party. One had the choice of either dropping by and going on to dinner or of making a meal of hors d'oeuvres. I was a "drop by and go out" kind of person, but the food that was on the buffet or that was being passed was always so tempting, that very often, I'd succumb.

Harry and I gave a huge party one time and I needed help, so I called a caterer. One of the trays they passed had chicken drumettes drenched in a delicious sauce, as well as napkins to go with them, but one lady spilled the sauce on her dress. She screamed so loud that you'd have thought a monster had bitten her on the leg. We of course offered to pay to have the dress cleaned, but she wanted to sue us for drippy hors d'oeuvres! I guess it must have been a really good dress.

Anyway, these wings aren't drippy—just tender and good. And I could make a meal of the mushrooms.

P.S. She didn't sue.

GLAZED CHICKEN WINGS

This recipe is from my friend Rose Ann Peterson.

25 chicken wings
½ cup soy sauce
½ cup dry sherry
4 tablespoons brown sugar
½ teaspoon ground ginger
4 green onions (white part only), cut in 1-inch lengths
1 cup water

Cut the tips from the chicken wings and disjoint. (Save the tips for stock.) Combine all of the ingredients in a large saucepan. Bring to a boil over medium-high heat. Simmer the wings for 1 hour and 30 minutes or until tender. Remove the wings from the liquid and let cool.

Glaze:
½ cup apricot jam
1 tablespoon vegetable oil
1 clove garlic, crushed
2 tablespoons soy sauce
½ teaspoon meat glaze (kitchen bouquet)

In a small bowl combine all of the glaze ingredients. Dip the wings into the mixture to coat. Arrange the wings on a broiler pan. Broil at least 5 inches from the heat for 5 minutes on one side. Turn over and baste with juices in the pan and broil for 5 minutes more. Serve at room temperature.
Makes 50.

BROILED STUFFED MUSHROOM CAPS

12 large white mushrooms
1   clove garlic, minced
3   shallots, minced
3   tablespoons butter
4   tablespoons olive oil
½   cup bread crumbs
½   cup grated Parmesan cheese
1   teaspoon basil
3   tablespoons chopped parsley
     Salt and fresh ground pepper

Preheat the oven to 350°. Clean the mushrooms, remove the stems, chop fine, and squeeze dry. In a saucepan over medium heat, sauté the garlic and shallots in 2 tablespoons of the butter and 1 tablespoon of the olive oil. Add the mushroom stems and stir over moderate heat until the liquid evaporates (approximately 5 minutes). Remove from the heat.

Mix the remaining ingredients. Adjust the seasonings to taste. Stuff the mushroom caps and top each with a dot of the remaining butter. Put in a shallow, well-oiled, ovenproof dish and bake for about 25 minutes. Serve hot.
Makes 12 caps.

Enjoying a cocktail party conversation with the lovely Barbara Eden.

Once More, With Feelllling!

I was in the danger zone again. Nearly every three years I had had a baby. But having gotten the message with James's epilepsy and Chris's lung problems, I knew that I should not have another.

In the fall, Chris, though only three, began going to pre-school because he was lonely at home without his brothers, and he was deemed ready. So now I had the morning hours to myself.

I had recently joined a women's charitable organization, Share, Inc., which raised money for developmentally disabled people. But I needed something more. So I decided to find a commercial agent and do some TV ads. Easier said than done.

It took tenacity through months of being rejected time and again to get an agent, but when I did, the first job I got was for a popular headache medicine. The scene was this: The husband comes home to his tense wife. She is cross with him and then pleads a bad headache—a really, really bad one. The husband gets her The Capsule and tah-dah, headache's gone, and are they cuddling once again. Terrific, right?

Well, the director was having a great time. When he was ready to shoot the big "Headache Closeup," he wanted me in real pain. "That's great," he said. "More." And again, "Now, a little more." And "You're really hurting! More! More! More!"

At the end of the day, he was beside himself with joy over this epic he had shot.

The commercial ran for about two weeks before the Federal Trade Commission forced the company to take the ad off the air because, the FTC said, The Capsule as shown purported to cure nervous breakdowns and insanity!

This full-meal salad is easy to make, and you'll get lots of compliments without a lot of headaches. I promise.

Getting everything just right for a food commercial.

CHICKEN POTATO SALAD

2   whole chicken breasts, poached,
      skinned, and boned
8   to 10 small red-skin potatoes, cooked
½   pound fresh green beans, cooked and
      cut into 1-inch pieces
1   small bunch scallions, chopped
2   or 3 ribs celery, chopped
6   to 8 fresh mushroom caps, cut in
      quarters

Dressing:
⅓   cup mayonnaise
⅓   cup sour cream
2   tablespoons red wine vinegar

1   tablespoon tarragon, chopped
      Salt and fresh cracked pepper to taste

Cube the skinned and boned chicken breasts. Cut the potatoes in half, or into quarters, depending on their size. Mix the potatoes with the beans, scallions, celery, and mushrooms. Add enough dressing to bind well.

Note: I never measure this. You can make it for 2 or for 20. Just use your judgment as to how much of each ingredient you want. Experiment!
Serves 4 to 6.

TAKING IT ON THE CHIN—Serving a delicious bite of the sponsor's product on the commercial set.

The Cat's Got My Tongue
(Or You Sneeze, You Lose)

Being the "new face" in town, I had good luck with commercials for the first year or so, and then it tailed off and got frustrating. The cutest one I did was for a cat food company in which my character exclaimed, "He's eating!!" People, total strangers, would pass me on the street and yell, "He's eating!!" I ran into actor/singer/director Gene Nelson one day in a restaurant. He yelled, "He's eating!!" My kids would say it all the time. It was crazy, but fun.

But one day, after a long, dry spell of not getting anything, I was in front of a small camera at an audition and sneezing for a cold remedy. That was it. Just sneezing. And I thought, "Wait a second here. This isn't what I want to do." That was the end of my commercial career.

This dish is wonderfully tasty. It was given to me by a friend at that time, Victoria Cutler, with whom I used to play at playing tennis. (She is the wife of screenwriter Stan Cutler.) We've lost track of each other, but she was a neat lady. This recipe seems too easy to be true, but it is. Serve it with garlic mashed potatoes and your favorite vegetable.

Victoria is Hungarian and doesn't believe that duck has to be all sauced up. I agree with her.

DUCKLING VICTORIA

1   duckling

Bake at 350° for 2 hours. Cut like chicken and bake until crispy.

A typical commercial pose—this one for tennis wear.

Being Sunny and Share

I had joined Share, Inc., in 1970 and of their two major fund-raisers each year, their variety show, "Boomtown," was the biggest. All of the members pitched in to help, as they do to this day.

Dancers danced and singers sang. There were menus to plan, decorating to do, items to prepare for auction, and arms of husbands, many of whom were entertainment superstars, to twist.

If it was decided that we needed paper flowers for a South of the Border theme, member Sonia Goodman taught us how to make them. There were no excuses. Woe be unto you if you didn't help out. As for flower making, I was hopeless. Sonia allowed me only to "crimp." That I could manage.

But dancing I could do better. And I loved it. Here I was, after all of those years, back in the chorus where I'd been so happy. The second year I was a member, Miriam

In the "Boomtown" show with Gloria Franks (center) and June Hutton.

Nelson (now Myers), a founder of Share, choreographed the show, which she did when her work schedule allowed.

This particular show had a '40s, World War II theme with a medley of songs and dances from *South Pacific,* plus a Hollywood Canteen section. Our favorite number was "Honey Bun," followed by "There's Nothing Like a Dame." It was great.

This isn't a honey bun, but it's the best coffee cake recipe I've ever made. Try it and you'll be hooked.

SOUR CREAM COFFEE CAKE

1½ cups cake flour
½ cup all-purpose flour
1 teaspoon baking soda
1 teaspoon baking powder
½ cup butter
½ cup sugar
1 egg, lightly beaten
1 teaspoon vanilla extract
1 cup sour cream
   Topping

All of the ingredients should be at room temperature. In a bowl mix together the flours, soda, and baking powder. In another bowl, cream together the

butter and the sugar until fluffy and light. Add the egg and vanilla and mix well. Add half of the dry ingredients, mixing just until the flour is blended. Blend in the sour cream and then the remaining dry ingredients.

Spread half of the batter lightly into a 10-inch tube pan. Sprinkle with half of the Topping and spread with the remaining batter. Sprinkle with the remaining Topping. Bake at 350° for 40 to 45 minutes.

Topping:
¼ cup all-purpose flour
¾ cup brown sugar, packed
¼ teaspoon salt
1 cup chopped walnuts
¼ cup butter

Mix together the flour, sugar, salt, and nuts. Add the butter in small pieces. Rub in by hand until the mixture is crumbly. Be careful not to overmix.
Makes 8 servings.

Learning the Charleston for the movie Tea for Two *more than three decades earlier paid off for me again as Roy Palmer and I brought the audience to their feet in a "Boomtown" show during the 1980s.*

Dances and Glances

Near the end of rehearsals during the last month before the Share show in May, they bring in extra dancers if they are needed—almost always males to partner the ladies. We could hardly have the Hollywood Canteen segment without them.

One afternoon in 1971, six guys came in the stage door at Goldwyn Studios, where we were rehearsing, and they ambled over to Miriam Nelson. We were all on break at the time, so we ladies, married though we were, looked them over. We began chumming around and looking for the ones we'd most like to dance with. Joan Benny Blumoff and I homed in on the same dancer. He was muscular, not tall, and Italian looking. He had a swagger of a walk and a nice smile. If he could dance, he'd suit us just fine.

We told Miriam that Joan and I would like for him to dance with us, as our parts in the show were already set, so we knew we could share one male dancer. After checking our heights against his (we were shorter than he), she acquiesced.

The dancer's name was Lou Genevrino and he was a wonderful dancer and very professional. We felt secure with

In the front row of a "Boomtown" show with Janet Leigh and Altovise Davis (Mrs. Sammy Davis, Jr.).

him on stage and each of us enjoyed his company during coffee breaks.

When the show ended after the usual one performance, Joan and I said goodbye to Lou. As he was from New York, we knew that he might never work in a Share show again. When I got to my car, there was a slip of paper tucked under the windshield wiper. It read, "Cuteness counts— Lou G."

Our paths were not to cross again for nearly twenty years.

These lamb shanks are awfully good and easy to prepare. It is a Yugoslavian way to prepare them—not Italian—but who cares when they're this tasty.

GHIVETCH (GOD BLESS YOU!)
(Lamb Shanks)

4	tomatoes
1½	cups peeled and diced eggplant
2	cups sliced zucchini
½	pound mushrooms, cut in halves
1	clove garlic, minced
1	bay leaf
¼	teaspoon thyme
¼	teaspoon basil
¼	teaspoon chopped parsley
	Salt and pepper to taste
4	small lamb shanks

Peel, seed, and quarter the tomatoes and combine them with the remaining ingredients, except the lamb shanks. Place the vegetables in a large casserole. Place the lamb shanks on top, cover, and bake at 325° for 3 hours, or until the meat is tender.
Serves 4.

A Tony-Winning Performance

I received a phone call one afternoon after the boys were home from school and busy with their homework. It was from a casting director connected with the Tony Randall and Jack Klugman series, *The Odd Couple.*

Having seen one of my commercials (though knowing I was pretty much retired), they wondered if I would like to do a very tiny part at the end of one of their episodes. I said sure; it'd be fun.

And it was—for the most part. Mr. Randall and Mr. Klugman couldn't have been nicer and the writer-director of the series (Neil Simon of course wrote the play from which the series sprung) Garry Marshall was very welcoming. But I hadn't really worked in a long time and my usual insecurity was at Mach 1.

This was also the first time that I had done a three- or four-camera show in front of an audience. It is a hybrid—not quite a play, because cameras are filming, and not quite pure film, because an audience responds with laughs, or heaven forbid, silence.

After the day of camera blocking was a dress rehearsal for all of the producers and writers—in complete wardrobe and not stopping unless the worst happened.

The worst happened.

Tony had named my character Miriam Welby (because by that time Robert Young was famous for playing Marcus Welby), and when Felix gave me my cue, I froze. Tony, who likes crisp pick-ups of lines (who doesn't!), started banging on the table we were sitting around—frantically yelling, "Say your line! Say your line!" I was so blank that I couldn't have said my own name.

Jack intervened, "Hey, Tony, relax. She'll say it. Give her a chance." Someone fed me my line and I tearfully made it to the end of the short scene. So much for my return to television.

The next day, when I came in to prepare for the night's filming, I found in my dressing room a beautiful, dainty floral arrangement with a sweet card welcoming me to the show—and apologizing. It was from Tony Randall.

I stayed with the show in a recurring role for over two seasons, and Tony and I got along like a house afire. Tony has very definite feelings about things and has no problem letting others know the score. To me, he is the ultimate soft-shell crab because he is sweetie underneath the bluster.

WILL MIRIAM MARRY HIM?— Tony Randall and I have a round-table discussion as boyfriend and girlfriend Felix Unger and Miriam Welby during a dress rehearsal for an episode of The Odd Couple.

BARBECUED SOFT-SHELL CRAB

12 dressed soft-shell blue crabs, fresh or frozen
¾ cup chopped parsley
½ cup melted fat or oil
1 teaspoon lemon juice
¼ teaspoon ground nutmeg
¼ teaspoon soy sauce
Dash liquid hot pepper sauce
Lemon wedges

Thaw the frozen crabs. Clean, wash, and dry the crabs. Place the crabs in well-greased, hinged wire grills. In a saucepan, combine the remaining ingredients except the lemon wedges. Heat. Baste the crabs with the sauce. Cook about 4 inches from moderately hot coals for 8 minutes. Baste with sauce and cook 7 to 10 minutes longer or until lightly browned. Serve with lemon wedges. *Serves 6.*

It was great fun working with Tony Randall and Jack Klugman on ABC-TV's The Odd Couple.

A Perfect Pair

I loved both Tony Randall and Jack Klugman. They worked so well off of each other. They were generous actors who were concerned with the whole show, rather than only themselves. They made it a wonderful set and probably the most pure fun that I'd had working in a long time. That is, except for the dress rehearsals. I never got over my fear of dress rehearsals.

Jack loved to bet on horses, and he and the prop men would listen to the racing results on a little radio in a tiny side room.

Harry and I would look at the race listings in the morning newspapers and make a game of choosing our horses. No money changed hands, but whoever had the most winners at the end of the race meet got a small treat of his or her choice. I'd arrive at the set, see the guys pouring over their racing papers, and tell them which ones I had bet on. One day, Jack, in frustration, asked "Whattaya—have a bookie in your house?"

Jack's most recent hit is on Broadway, where he has been starring with Tony Randall in *The Sunshine Boys.* He sent his spaghetti sauce recipe from there. By the way, Jack sometimes visits friends who operate Hollywood Pizza in Hendersonville, Tennessee, just outside of Nashville. Every once in a while, a lucky customer might spot Jack tossing a handmade pizza in the back during one of his visits to the area.

JACK KLUGMAN'S ITALIAN SAUCE

¼	cup olive oil
10	cloves garlic, pressed
1	pound Italian sausage
2	to 3 pounds pork butt with bone
3	28-ounce cans Italian plum tomatoes
1	16-ounce can tomato purée
1	6-ounce can tomato paste
½	cup water
	Basil
	Oregano
	Parsley
	Salt and pepper to taste

In a skillet, brown the garlic in the oil. Then brown the meats. Add the tomato items and about ½ cup of water. Bring to a boil and then simmer, while adding the seasonings. Simmer for 2 hours, stirring often and adjusting the seasonings to taste. Enjoy!

The happy face of the delightful Al Molinaro.

Murray Knows Cooking

Al Molinaro played Murray Greshner, the lovable cop on *The Odd Couple.* In speaking with Al recently, he told me that he has been writing. He gave up acting and doesn't miss it at all. He was writing for films and for television at Paramount for a while and he has just completed a book of short stories. He may not miss television, but we miss him.

About this recipe, Al says, "Wouldn't you know it would be something my mother used to cook for our family of ten children. I was number nine in the pecking order. It reflects back to the days when my parents were not doing very well during the Depression, and they had to really cut corners. To this day, whenever I'm left alone to make a meal for myself, I resort to my own Pasta E Fagioli. As my Grandma used to say, 'Try it. You'll like it.'"

AL MOLINARO'S FAMILY PASTA E FAGIOLI
(MACARONI AND BEAN SOUP)

2   cups dried Cannellini beans
1   small piece prosciutto rind or bacon
      rind (about ¼ pound)
1   large onion, chopped
2   large garlic cloves, minced
¼   cup olive oil
1   small potato, peeled and cubed
10 cups water
1   cup canned tomatoes, drained
      Salt and pepper to taste
      Garlic salt
8   ounces ditalini or pasta shells, cooked
      and drained
6   to 8 heaping tablespoons grated
      Parmesan cheese

Soak the beans overnight in cold water, changing the water several times.

Cook the rind in boiling water for 2 minutes, then rinse under cold water. Cut the rind into small pieces. In a skillet heat the oil and sauté the onion and garlic, being careful not to burn the garlic or it will become bitter. Add the drained beans that have been soaking, potatoes, and water. Add the tomatoes and the rind. Cover and simmer over low-to-moderate heat for 45 minutes or until the beans are tender. Taste and add any necessary seasonings.

Add the drained pasta and cook for an additional 10 to 12 minutes.

Allow to cool and then sprinkle with Parmesan cheese and black pepper.
Serves 4.

Something was always making somebody laugh on The Odd Couple. *It's all I can do not to break out laughing at the wrong time when doing this scene with Tony Randall's Felix Unger. Penny Marshall and Al Molinaro were luckier. Their characters obviously were* supposed *to be laughing.*

Producer/writer/director/actor extraordinaire and just all-around nice man Garry Marshall.

Happy Ways

Talk about generous! Garry Marshall is one of the most generous producer/writer/directors in all of Hollywood. And loyal. He loves actors, he loves show business completely, and he is a prolific talent. He plays the drums, he does hilarious standup comedy, and he even acts in movies and television now.

Of course, Garry was executive producer for *The Odd Couple.* And years later, I was delighted when he gave me the role of Bridget, the nice saleslady in *Pretty Woman.* But I was even more delighted when the film became an overnight sensation for him and his stars. It couldn't have happened to a nicer man.

Garry and his wife, Barbara, have a large family. (You may not know it, but Barbara always has a cameo in any of his films. For example, she was Mrs. Ramey, the customer I was saying goodbye to in the background of my scene with Julia Roberts in *Pretty Woman.* And she was a nun in *Dear God,* the recent film starring Greg Kinnear.)

Barbara gave me this recipe over the phone. Like most of us, she doesn't measure, but this is Garry's favorite dish.

CHICKEN PASTA GARRY MARSHALL

2   chicken breasts skinned and boned
      and cut into 2-inch pieces
1   large onion, chopped
2   tablespoons olive oil
2   cups tomato puree
2   cups Ragu
1   cup frozen peas
      Angel hair pasta

In a large skillet heat the olive oil over medium to medium-high heat and sauté the chicken and onions until the onions are transparent and the chicken is cooked through (that is, it's no longer pink inside). Add the sauces and bring to a low simmer. Add the peas and reheat. Cook the pasta as you like it and serve with sauce over it.

Making the
Most of Life's
Stages

Downsizing

There were good things happening and some not so good.

The best were the children. Susan was now happily married and a mother of three. Steve had graduated from college. Brian was attending college and doing better than he'd ever done in grade or high school. Peter was a delight with his hobby of magic and mimicry. James, who pushed himself, had been, mercifully, seizure-free for a year or more, and Chris was a cutie-pie, my baby.

Harry enjoys a magazine in his leisure chair.

But since *Ugliest Girl in Town* some seven years before, Harry's long and illustrious career had taken a slide. He had gone from Columbia/Screen Gems after a cruel termination, then to Hanna-Barbera to do heaven only knows what, and then to Paramount for a short and frustrating stint in smaller and smaller offices.

We were forced to sell the house, take the boys out of private schools, sell some items, and pull in our horns. It was the order of the day from our business manager.

Harry was afraid to break the news to me, except that I knew he wasn't happy at these new studios. He'd kept up a pretense that everything was the same as always. Because we had a business manager, I never saw a bill. I hadn't a clue as to what was going on with our financial lives.

But when he told me, I encouraged the change. It was a perfect time. James was to graduate in June from the sixth grade at the John Thomas Dye School. Peter was to enter Notre Dame High School in the fall. Brian lived at college and Chris was to start the third grade and was young enough to be adaptable. Better now than later, I said.

And so the preparations began.

Comfort food is very important in times of stress. They give me a sense of stability and security. This was one of ours. My stepdaughter Susan said that I had to put it in the book.

EGG NOODLES WITH TUNA (OR SALMON)

1   8 ounce-package American Beauty egg
       noodles, cooked
1½ cups cottage cheese
1½ cups sour cream
½   cup finely chopped onion
1   clove garlic, minced
2   teaspoons Worcestershire sauce
½   teaspoon salt
¼   teaspoon pepper
     Dash Tabasco

1   6½-ounce can tuna or salmon
       (drained or flaked)
½   cup grated sharp cheese

Place the noodles in a buttered casserole dish. Combine all of the ingredients except cheese and blend well. Pour over the egg noodles. Toss lightly to mix the sauce with the noodles. Sprinkle with grated cheese. Bake at 325° for 40 minutes.
Serves 6 to 8.

Garage Sale Fever

We put the house on the market and it sold within a week for twice what we'd paid ten years before. We were glad about that and began looking for a smaller place near the boys' schools. When we found it and made plans to move, we knew we had to get rid of an accumulation of possessions, so we had a garage sale.

Reluctant at first, Harry really got into the swing of things when he saw the crowd gathering, and we had a brisk two-day sale. It was a little too brisk for me.

I had a collection of dolls, not a large one, but well-made stuffed animal kinds of things that meant a lot to me. Chris and James came up to me on Saturday afternoon and handed me a ten-dollar bill. They proudly told me that since I hadn't put them out they'd decided to take my dolls in their wagon door-to-door in the neighborhood and sell them for me.

On Sunday afternoon, as the sale was winding down, I escaped to take a hot bath when I heard adult voices in our dressing room. Harry was so caught up in the selling thing that he was offering my Indian jewelry to a late-arriving dealer.

"Wait, wait!" I hollered, and quickly throwing on a robe found the two of them poring over the items Harry had now put out on the dining room table. Needless to say, we declined to sell.

Here is a made-up peach dessert from one summer when a friend gave us a lot of home-grown peaches. It is a cozy dish and very similar to one my mother made when I was little.

DANISH PEACH CRUMBLE

4	fresh peaches		¼	cup butter
¾	cup sugar		¾	cup all-purpose flour
1	tablespoon all-purpose flour		½	cup sugar
1	teaspoon lemon juice		2	large almond macaroons, crumbled
½	teaspoon ground nutmeg			

Peel the peaches and slice thinly. Mix with the sugar, flour, lemon juice, and nutmeg, and let sit while you prepare the topping.

In a small bowl combine the butter, flour, sugar, and macaroons, and mix until crumbly. Put the peaches in a buttered 8-inch square Pyrex dish and spread the topping over all. Bake at 375° for 40 to 50 minutes.
Serves 4 to 6.

I prove to be pretty peachy as a demonstrator at my after-school job while I try to earn enough money to buy a new dress for a school ball in this 1955 episode of Father Knows Best.

Family Reunion

Lo and behold, just as we were deep in plans to move, a big project came up for me. There was to be a television reunion movie of *Father Knows Best* in the spring of 1977.

Bill Gray and I spoke on the phone, and we had mixed feelings about it. We had a great fear of stepping backward—worried that the show would seem tired or sad.

There was a script reading scheduled a week or so before rehearsals began, and it would be the first time we had all been together in nearly twenty years. We gathered in a board room on the Warner Bros. lot in Burbank and greeted each other with semi-false bonhomie. But where was Mr. Young? We'd heard that he had arrived. We'd seen his wife, Betty, in the hallway, but where could he be? Apparently, we found out later, he was so anxious about the project that he was hiding in the men's room!

Robert Young and Betty, his future wife, met during this high school play when he was sixteen and she was fourteen.

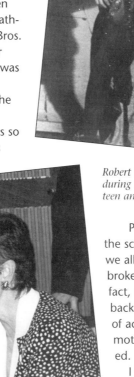

Robert Young and I visit at his ninetieth birthday party.

Presently we began the reading of the script and when we were finished, we all laughed and joked—the ice was broken and we were "family" again. In fact, rather than it feeling like a step backward, it had a wonderful feeling of acceptance of the past and forward motion. We couldn't wait to get started.

I had the privilege of visiting with Mr. Young in early 1998 at his home in Westlake, California, and a friend of his, Gayle Fredericks, gave me this recipe that Betty, his now-deceased wife, used to make for him.

DUCK SOUP

	Leftover duck carcass
1	bay leaf
4	cups water
1	onion, chopped
	Celery leaves
½	cup finely chopped onion
½	cup finely chopped celery
1	tablespoon parsley
1	teaspoon thyme
1	tablespoon salt
	Pepper to taste
1	cup Madeira
1	apple, peeled and grated
	Consommé

In a large saucepan simmer the duck, bay leaf, water, onion, and celery leaves for 1 hour. Strain and cool and skim off the fat.

In a large skillet melt the butter and sauté the onion and celery until brown. Add the parsley, thyme, salt, and pepper. Add the dark meat stripped from the bones, Madeira, and apple. If more liquid is needed, add the consommé. Cook for 1 hour.
Serves 4.

DOCTOR ON CALL—Robert Young as Marcus Welby, M.D.

A New TV Family

On top of the *Father Knows Best* TV movie came another offer. Paramount and producer-writer Joanna Lee were doing a script of hers for NBC called *Mulligan's Stew,* and I was wanted to play the mother of a family who inherits the husband's brother's family at his untimely death. On TV, parents and lots of children, some not their own, have always reaped comedic benefits, and so the network was very high on this idea.

The last day of the *Father Knows Best* shoot was on April 19, 1977. Our move from the big house to the little one was on April 19. And the first day of filming *Mulligan's Stew* began early in the morning on location in Brentwood on April 20. As the boys would say when quoting Gilda Radner's *Saturday Night Live* persona Rosanne Rosanna-Dana, "It's always something."

Remember when Harry left for England when I was expecting Chris? I think I got my revenge.

Since nothing was unpacked (and for days and days it remained that way), we went out to dinner to celebrate my birthday and also our anniversary that would be two days later on the 21st. We went to St. Germaine, a fine French restaurant that no longer exists. This was one of my favorite things to have there.

Lawrence Pressman and I play a new dad and mom to our own three and a bunch of orphans on NBC's Mulligan's Stew *sitcom.*

MUSHROOM SALAD ST. GERMAINE

Vinaigrette:

3   tablespoons red wine vinegar
2   tablespoons Dijon mustard
1   cup olive oil
      Dash dry white wine
      Salt and fresh ground pepper to taste

Salad:

1   pound large white mushrooms
      Juice of ½ lemon
2   tablespoons chopped parsley
2   tablespoons chopped chives
      Tomatoes for garnish

In a blender blend the vinegar and mustard. Gradually add the oil until the mixture thickens. Add the white wine and salt and pepper. This makes 1½ cups.

Slice the mushrooms. Sprinkle with the lemon juice. Add the parsley, chives, and vinaigrette and combine well. Chill.

On butter lettuce spoon the mushroom salad and garnish with tomato slices or cherry tomatoes.

Serves 4.

The Mulligan's Stew family: Surrounding Lawrence Pressman and me are (clockwise from top left) are Chris Ciampa, Lory Kochheim, Julie Anne Haddock, Johnny Doran, K.C. Martel, Suzanne Crough, and Sunshine Lee.

Out of Stew

As everything always does, life finally settled down into a routine. Slowly we got unpacked as I finished the TV movie for NBC.

The male star was Lawrence Pressman, a handsome and personable actor who has great skill at both comedy and drama. He was wonderful to work with, committed to his craft and yet friendly and warm.

Mulligan's Stew aired that summer without much fanfare. Larry and I had had nice careers, but we were hardly household names.

NBC was shocked and elated when, wonder of wonders, the ratings went through the roof. They wanted a series and they wanted it for fall. Forget that it takes months to properly prepare story lines and scripts for a weekly film series; we could do it and we must. So, Joanna Lee put her nose to the grindstone and tried the impossible: to ready a full order for a one-hour comedy series in six weeks. It was a noble effort, but one that was doomed to fail. We were only on the air for four weeks when NBC pulled the plug.

One of the guests on the show was actress Beulah Quo. As there is always a lot of sitting around time on film sets, we'd get to chatting about this and that and eventually it nearly always led to a discussion of food. She shared this with me then, and I share it with you now.

POPPY SEED CAKE
(From the kitchen of Beulah Quo)

1   18¼-ounce package Duncan Hines yellow cake mix
4   eggs
½   cup oil
½   cup sherry (inexpensive)
1   3-ounce package instant vanilla pudding
½   pint sour cream
⅓   cup poppy seeds

In a large bowl combine all of the ingredients and mix thoroughly. Pour into a greased bundt or tube pan. Bake at 350°for 50 minutes to 1 hour.
Serves 8.

Kentucky Delight

Lawrence Pressman is so talented. He works nearly all the time and co-starred in one of my favorite shows, *Doogie Howser, M.D.,* as Dr. Canfield. He is from the South and with Southern graciousness he shares this recipe with you.

"This recipe is a Southern staple. It comes from my hometown of Cynthiana, Kentucky. My mother and most Southern ladies have this one to serve with the turkey at Thanksgiving or the Kentucky ham at Christmas or with both at both. As my mother would have said, 'It's deee-lish.' Y'all enjoy."—Lawrence Pressman

Lawrence Pressman and me during Mulligan's Stew *days.*

MY MOTHER ROSE'S CORN PUDDING

6   **tablespoons butter**
2   **tablespoons sugar**
2   **tablespoons all-purpose flour**
1   **teaspoon salt**
4   **eggs**
2   **cups fresh corn (if using canned, makes sure it's thoroughly rinsed and drained)**
1½ **cups milk or half and half (depends on how custardy one wants; half and half makes it much richer, and I recommend it)**

In a large bowl blend the butter, sugar, flour, and salt. Add the eggs, beating well. Slowly stir in the corn and then the milk. Pour the ingredients in a buttered casserole dish. Bake at 325° for 45 minutes. Only stir once during baking.

When done, the pudding will be golden brown on top and have a custard consistency inside. Let stand until room temperature before cutting. It can be warmed just before serving.

Serves 4.

No More Stewing

My favorite picture of James, at age five.

Well, here I was not working and getting paid for the unshot episodes of *Mulligan's Stew,* and now it seemed as though we could have stayed in the big house a while longer. Not only that, but real estate values took a big jump in the years following and at its last sale, our old house was on the market for well over a million dollars. One of our sons has never quite forgiven me!

The most wonderful thing that occurred during this time was that Dr. Podosin, James' neurologist, after tests and careful examination, determined that we should try very, very slowly to wean James off of his epilepsy medicine. He felt that James, at twelve, was due for a big growth spurt, which would help, and he also didn't want him to start a new school carrying the burden of what was perceived as a disability.

With our hearts in our mouths, we began to cut back the dosage. James has said that as he began taking fewer and fewer pills it was as though a fog was clearing. He hadn't realized how poorly he'd felt until he began to feel better. Gratefully the seizures never returned. After high school he had a distinguished few years in the United States Coast Guard and he is now a television executive based in London, England, married and the father of two children.

JAMES ACKERMAN'S SAUCE-FOR-A-WEEK

1   pound ground veal
2   medium or 1 very large onion, chopped
8   cloves garlic, pressed or very finely minced
2   to 3 tablespoons olive oil
     Rosemary to taste
     Thyme to taste
     Salt and pepper to taste
4   28-ounce cans whole tomatoes, broken up
1   cup red wine

In a skillet brown the meat, onion, and garlic in the olive oil. Add the seasonings and blend. Pour in the tomatoes and break up the large pieces. Add the red wine and cook with the pot's lid slightly ajar for 2 to 3 hours or until nicely thickened. Serve over spaghetti or pasta of your choice.
Serves 8, at least.

Dancing on the Clouds

Soon I was taping a TV special, *The Family and Other Living Things*—singing and dancing with Bill Bixby. The only problem was that Bill couldn't dance and I couldn't sing.

The director was Robert Shearer, who, as a teenager, had tap-danced and played the drums in my first movie, *Mr. Big*. He was soon to be an Emmy winner for his directorial achievements.

Shearer staged the number that we did with "son" Brad Savage on elaborate risers or steps, with platforms going everywhere. It was no big deal, except that the steps were open to the ground like wide ladders and they went wa-a-ay up high. Try that some time when you're nervous about your singing or dancing.

Since this was a "mom and apple pie" kind of show, I'm going to give you a mom's apple pie from my neighbor Peggy Ramey. Yes, that's where Garry Marshall and I got the name of Barbara Marshall's character in *Pretty Woman,* remember?

Bill Bixby, Brad Savage, and me—we are family.

APPLE CRUMB PIE

1	9-inch pie crust
4	to 5 large tart apples
½	cup sugar
1	teaspoon ground cinnamon
½	cup sugar
¾	cup all-purpose flour
⅓	cup butter

Preheat the oven to 400°. Line a 9-inch pie pan with the pastry. Pare the apples and arrange in the pan. Sprinkle with sugar mixed with cinnamon. In a medium bowl sift the remaining sugar with the flour. Cut in the butter until crumbly. Sprinkle over the apples. Bake for 10 minutes, and then reduce heat to 350° and bake for about 40 minutes or until the apples are tender. *Serves 6 to 8.*

Going with the Flow

Football, tennis, jogging, and deep-sea fishing had taken a toll on Harry's body. Not only did he have knee problems, but severe back pain now plagued him daily. He had tried everything until Dr. Marshall Urist at UCLA presented him with his choices. And while one choice was the most drastic, it offered the opportunity for a full and complete recovery. It was surgery, a double laminectomy and fusion, a procedure in which new bone is used to replace damaged bones.

Peter was now old enough to watch over himself. James helped look after Chris, and Mother, who'd moved two blocks from us, watched over everybody, while I worked and visited UCLA.

I'd had a strange experience in the spring of 1979 on a pilot for a series called *Highcliffe Manor,* starring Shelley Fabares. I was fired by NBC after the first table reading. Then, while Harry was in the hospital recovering, I was rehired only to be let go a week later—again—on the night of the dreaded dress rehearsal. Yes, that again!

But I went on to do the first of three episodes over the years for Aaron Spelling's *The Love Boat* and what fun they were. Mr. Spelling spared no expense when it came to clothing his actors. He knew, just as Jean-Louis at Columbia had believed years before, that when you feel good about yourself and how you look, it shows on screen—even down to the most beautiful shoes and handbags.

Jeraldine Saunders created the concept of *The Love Boat* from her book of that name and she is a woman who is as beautiful inside as she is out. And that is saying something. This is her recipe.

Jeraldine Saunders is the beautiful lady responsible for launching The Love Boat.

LOVE BOAT ENERGY DOLLOPS

2	cups unsweetened carob powder
2	tablespoons ground cinnamon
1	teaspoon ground nutmeg
½	cup dry milk powder (optional)
2	cups chopped walnuts
1½	pounds peanut butter
1	cup whole raw milk

In a large bowl mix the dry ingredients together well. Add the peanut butter and milk. Form into balls about the size of Ping-Pong balls or smaller. Do not cook. Eat as is. These are also good frozen, and are finger-licking good.

Love that Ted

One of the most delightful gentlemen in Hollywood is Ted Lange. He made his name on *Love Boat* but went on to become a sought-after director in television as well as theater. He also writes many plays that he directs to great critical success.

He is famous for his candied yams. We thank him and his family for letting him share this treat with us.

The Love Boat's *Ted Lange is a lovely guy.*

TEDDY'S CANDIED YAMS

6	to 7 yams
	Ground cinnamon
	Ground nutmeg
½	cup margarine or butter
1	cup firmly packed brown sugar
	Juice of 1 lemon
	Juice of 1 orange
	Marshmallows

Cut the yams in half and boil. (By cutting them in half you speed up the cooking process.) Poke with a fork and when you are able to penetrate easily, the yams are done.

Rinse the yams and peel when cooled. Slice the yams length-wise and place in an oblong baking dish. Sprinkle liberally with cinnamon. Sprinkle less liberally with nutmeg. Cut the butter into chunks and place throughout the dish. Crumble the brown sugar across the yams. Squeeze the lemon and orange juices onto the yams. Bake at 350° for 20 minutes, occasionally mixing the yam mixture. Remove from the oven and place the marshmallows on the top. Bake until the marshmallows are melted and brown.

Peter Acts Up

After a long recuperation, Harry's back was on the mend. One of the first times—I think *the* first time—he was out of the house after surgery, was to see Peter in his first high school production. It was The Sound of Music, and he was playing Rolfe, the young Gestapo officer who sings "I am sixteen, going on seventeen."

Peter, Marie, and son Harry III in a happy family portrait.

Peter sing? I'd never heard a peep out of him; a very quiet and self-contained boy he was. Like most teens, Peter usually communicated to us with indistinguishable grunts to our queries. Sing? No way. Me, nervous? You better believe it.

The production was excellent, done in conjunction with an all-girls' Catholic school, Corvallis, and the all-boys equivalent, Notre Dame High. The staging was professional and the casting of all the roles was superior. Then the big moment came and Peter entered the stage in his messenger's uniform and began to sing.

He had a clear, light baritone voice, and his concentration on stage was such that you believed him totally as that young man. The hairs on my arms stood up and when glancing at Harry, we both had tears welling up in our eyes. Oh, nuts, another actor in the family. He was good.

Peter continued throughout high school and college to pursue that dream, did a bit of television work, won some theater awards, and then made a decision. He left show business for a more stable life with wife Marie and two children and is now happily in property management.

Peter shares my taste for Southwestern dishes, and I could sneak this one past his father, who didn't. I liked to make it for family get-togethers, and it is wonderful with steak, chops, or chicken.

CHILI RICE CASSEROLE

3   cups cooked long grain white rice
    Salt and freshly ground pepper to
      taste
3   cups sour cream
1   teaspoon salt
1   7-ounce can diced green chilies
¾   pound Monterey Jack cheese, cut in
    strips
½   cup grated Cheddar cheese

Preheat the oven to 350°. Butter a 1½-quart casserole. Season the rice with salt and pepper. Combine sour cream, salt, and chilies. In the prepared casserole, place a layer of rice, cover with a layer of the sour cream mixture, and top with strips of Monterey Jack cheese. Repeat, making 2 or 3 layers and ending with rice on top. Bake for 40 to 45 minutes or until heated through.

Sprinkle with grated Cheddar cheese and return to the oven until the cheese is melted.

Murder in Florida

On returning for a second *Love Boat* appearance, Gavin MacLeod, the beloved captain, asked if I'd like to do a play with him in St. Petersburg, Florida, that coming summer. It was *Murder Among Friends,* which had starred Janet Leigh and Jack Cassidy when it played on Broadway. Of course, my answer was a resounding yes.

We had a great cast, including Elmarie Wendel, a talented comedienne who's now regularly seen on *3rd Rock From the Sun;* and Rafael Ferrer, the young son of Jose Ferrer and Rosemary Clooney. The cast was rounded out by delightful character actor Larry Kogut and newcomer Russell Scott.

I adored Florida. It's one of those places that looks like itself; you know where you are. I even loved the summer humidity. Our apartments were in a complex, which Gavin dubbed Beer Can Villas, that was adjacent to a swamp whose squeaking, thumping creature sounds reverberating during the night seemed very exotic to me.

Russell Scott's family was from the area, and his mother, Mary, gave me this recipe, which I have used ever since. I think you'll like it too.

Gavin MacLeod and I share center stage in Murder Among Friends, *with Russell Scott in the background.*

SOUTHERN PECAN PIE

Pastry:
1⅓ cups all-purpose flour
½ teaspoon salt
½ cup Crisco
3 tablespoons of ice water

Combine all of the pastry ingredients to make a dough, then roll out to make a crust, and place in a 9-inch pie pan.

Filling:
1 cup white corn syrup
1 cup light brown sugar
¼ cup melted butter
  Pinch salt
3 eggs, slightly beaten
1¼ cups pecan halves
1 teaspoon vanilla extract

Preheat the oven to 350°. Combine all of the ingredients, blend well, and pour into the unbaked pie shell. Bake for 45 to 50 minutes. This pie is very rich, so small servings are in order.
Serves 8 to 10.

Tribute to Howie

Our director was Howard Morris, whom TV fans know from *Your Show of Shows* with Sid Caesar and *The Andy Griffith Show,* among many other credits. He did a fine job guiding us because critics and audiences alike were very complimentary.

Howie and I even worked together the following year at the same theater, only this time Howie was the star, not the director, in *Tribute,* a Neil Simon comedy.

I doubt this Blintz Casserole is on his diet, as it is very rich, but oh so good. For Sunday brunch with fresh fruit, it can't be beat. This was given me by hair stylist Cary Wisner, and it and she are jewels.

BLINTZ CASSEROLE

1½ cups sour cream
4   eggs
¼   cup sugar
1   teaspoon vanilla extract
½   cube butter, melted
2   boxes of cheese blintzes

Preheat the oven to 400°. In a bowl beat together the sour cream, eggs, sugar, and vanilla. Spread half of the butter in the bottom of a casserole. Lay the blintzes in the casserole and the pour mixture over them. Drizzle the rest of the butter on top. Bake for 55 minutes. It's done when golden brown. Serve with stewed fruit, applesauce, strawberry jam, or cherry preserves.

The cast for Murder Among Friends *at St. Petersburg's Country Dinner Playhouse included, clockwise from top left, Russell Scott, Rafael Ferrer, Elmarie Wendel, Larry Kogut, me, director Howard Morris, and Gavin MacLeod.*

Pretty in Pink

After the play was up and running, my free time was spent seeing the sights. I adored St. Petersburg Beach and especially the Don CeSar Hotel. But when I stayed closer to home, I'd visit the Sunken Gardens and see the flamingos.

Harry and I swooned over this dessert that we frequently had at a favorite restaurant of ours, The Oyster House. Sadly, it no longer exists, but before it closed we were able to get their very, very easy recipe for Flamingo Pie!

FLAMINGO PIE

1⅓ cups lemon juice
2 pounds creamed cheese, softened
1 14-ounce can sweetened condensed
    milk
1 cup sugar
2 egg yolks, beaten
2 to 3 drops of red food coloring
2 8-inch graham cracker crusts

Whip the lemon juice into softened cream cheese. Add the milk, sugar, and yolks. Put in the food coloring until a nice shade of pale pink develops. Pour into prepared graham cracker crust(s) and chill until set. Top with slightly sweetened thick whipped cream, if desired.
Makes 2 8-inch pies or 1 10-inch pie.

The Don CeSar Hotel

Nursing Around

In 1984 I was hired to act for three days on the popular soap opera *Days of Our Lives.* I was to play the evil Nurse Honeycutt, and those three days stretched into two years, except for a short time in the middle. I'll explain.

My character had been very naughty and was being punished, and fans were interested in the outcome. I was standing in a line one day when a young woman standing one person behind me (an elderly gentleman was between us), called out, "Hey, Nurse Honeycutt, where have you been?"

I began to tell her that I had been sent to prison for trying to kill Marlena in her hospital bed, but that I was out now and she'd be seeing me soon. The older gentleman was cringing behind me and creeping away from the line with fear in his eyes when we let him know that we were talking "daytime TV."

I remember a lot of people I worked with over the years while on *Days*. Patsy Pease, who'd played my daughter in the play *The Pleasure of His Company,* and Lana Saunders, Larry Pressman's wife, who was playing Sister Marie on the soap, were two.

Two new friends were made: beautiful and gracious Diedre Hall, and dear Suzanne Rogers, whose warmth, humor, twinkling eyes, and bright smile would light up anyone's day. Her devotion to God radiates from her and I am proud to call her a friend.

Suzanne Rogers.

CHICKEN BRUNSWICK STEW
(From Suzanne Rogers)

1	ham hock
1	large onion, cut up
2	ribs celery, cut up
1	whole chicken, skinned and cut in pieces
1	large can peeled tomatoes
1	cup corn
1	cup frozen butter beans
2	large potatoes, peeled and cut into 1-inch cubes
	Salt and pepper to taste
	Pat butter or margarine (optional)

Place the ham hock in a medium saucepan and cover with water. Add the onion and celery. Boil for approximately 30 minutes to obtain stock. Place the chicken in the saucepan and cook for about 1 hour until the chicken comes loose from the bones.

Remove the chicken from the saucepan and place in a bowl to cool. Put the tomatoes, corn, and butter beans in the stock and let boil for about 45 minutes.

Add the potatoes and let boil for about 10 minutes. While the stew is boiling down, take the chicken off the bones and tear into small pieces. Add the chicken to the stew, and remove the ham hock. Turn the stew to low and simmer for several hours.

Add salt and pepper to taste You may add a pat of butter or margarine, if desired. Also, if you wish, you may add another small can of tomatoes.
Serves 6.

Soap Days of My Life

If any of you have gotten hooked on the soaps, you'll know how complicated the plots can sometimes be. My whole time on *Days* seemed to revolve around the "The Prism." I never saw it for it was always being stolen, hidden, or transported from one place to the next. I never even knew the significance of it, just that it was really important.

Nearly fifteen years ago I had to learn this line—and once learned, never forgotten. It goes like this:

> (Whispered very fast) "Carleton learned that poachers, who were selling endangered species skins, found The Prism in the belly of an alligator they killed!"

At lunch break the actors eat lightly because a long afternoon is ahead with a dress rehearsal and taping to follow, so salads, fresh fruit, and vegetables are consumed by the caseload.

This is a wonderful dip for veggies that was given me by yet another hair stylist, this time a studio gal who'd been with *The Love Boat* crew for years. This is a staple at parties, and requests for the recipe are always made.

NAOMI'S DILL DIP

1   small carton sour cream
     Equal parts mayonnaise
2   tablespoons finely chopped parsley
2   tablespoons finely chopped green
     onions
1   teaspoon Beau Monde
1   teaspoon dill weed

In a serving bowl mix all of the ingredients together. Refrigerate overnight.

Serve with cauliflower, zucchini, mushrooms, celery, etc.

The evil Nurse Honeycutt on Days of Our Lives.

Never Give Up

Harry never gave up. He had an indomitable spirit. If the television business didn't want him, he'd do something else. So in his late sixties he went to real estate school and got his California license. And while he gallantly pursued that for a couple of years, his heart wasn't in it, and he kept trying to connect with another TV hit.

At last, with a young man named Ralph Riskin, he presented and got an order to do *The New Gidget* for first-run syndication. Not only that, but he was presented with a star on the Hollywood Walk of Fame. As luck would have it, I was in Canada doing a play with Tom Poston and couldn't attend his ceremony, but he was so proud he nearly burst his buttons.

Harry's happy hour when he got his star on the Hollywood Walk of Fame. Celebrating with him are (left to right) Caryn Richman, Johnny Grant (the mayor of Hollywood), Harry, Bill Welsh, and Dean Butler.

At the age of seventy-three he was on top of the world again and the newest jewel in his crown was *The New Gidget.* The cast was superb with Caryn Richman as Gidget and Dean Butler as her husband. Sidney Penny and William Schallert rounded out the cast, and many episodes were directed expertly by Ted Lange of *Love Boat* fame.

Harry's star, should you ever visit, is just a foot or so east of the entrance of his very favorite restaurant, Musso and Frank. He got to choose his spot and that one won hands down.

As I've mentioned, though he was a well-traveled and sophisticated man, Harry truly preferred comfort food and he was crazy about corn on the cob.

This is a fantastic preparation. It's great for serving a crowd or a couple, it takes the guesswork out, and is always perfect.

PEGGY'S CORN

For as many ears of corn as you will serve, have ready:

Softened butter
Dampened sheet of paper towel
Square of foil, the same size as towel

The day of the meal, shuck the corn and generously butter each ear. Put each ear diag-onally on a damp paper towel and roll up, tucking in the edges as you go. Then, do the same with the foil squares. If done ahead, just refrigerate until 1 hour before use. Preheat the oven to 400°; put the foil-covered ears on a baking sheet, and roast for 20 minutes.

Harry and me at home.

Adventures in Canada

Home again! But not for long. Back to Canada I went six months or so later to do a series for the first season of Barry Diller's new TV network, Fox Broadcasting.

It was exciting to be part of something so fresh and innovative. The show was called *The New Adventures of Beans Baxter* and starred young actor Jonathan Ward, with Scott Bremner playing his little brother, and guess who I was? You win. I played Mom.

The show was conceived by a tall, good-looking wild man who came by his name naturally, Savage Steve Holland. He kept us hopping and busy and it was enormous fun.

We shot in Vancouver, British Columbia, and that was reason enough to enjoy it. Jonathan's mother and I (when I had time) would explore, and once flew by helicopter to Vancouver Island for the day.

To honor Vancouver's British heritage, I'd like to present this rarebit recipe. It was served in Los Angeles at the old Cock & Bull, a small, cozy pub-like place on Sunset Boulevard, just up the block from Scandia that, sadly, is also no longer there. Many a happy time was spent there, and at least we have this recipe to remember it by.

WELSH RAREBIT

1	tablespoon butter
1	cup beer
1	pound sharp Cheddar cheese, grated
1	egg
1	teaspoon Worcestershire sauce
½	teaspoon salt
4	drops hot pepper sauce
¼	teaspoon curry powder
¼	teaspoon dry mustard
1	teaspoon chopped chives
6	slices bread, toasted
	Halved hard-boiled eggs, optional
	Quartered tomatoes, optional

In a 2-quart saucepan melt the butter over low heat. Blend in the beer. Add the cheese and stir constantly over low heat until smooth. Beat the egg in a bowl and add a few spoonfuls of hot cheese mixture and blend well. Blend the egg mixture into the remaining cheese mixture, stirring constantly. Add the Worcestershire sauce, salt, hot pepper sauce, curry powder, mustard, and chives, and cook over low heat, stirring frequently, for 10 minutes. Serve over toast and garnish with halved hard-cooked eggs and quartered tomatoes.
Serves 6.

Laughing with director Savage Steve Holland (third from left) and friends in Vancouver.

THE RACE IS ON—Gordon Liddy guest starred in one episode of The New Adventures of Beans Baxter.

Changing Spots Again

Life has its curves. That summer and fall couldn't have been better. Harry had a hit show in syndication. I had a show on a new network. Steve, Susan, and Brian had been married, and now Peter and Marie tied the knot at a formal afternoon ceremony that I flew in for in the morning and out again at night. Exciting times.

To allow the crew of *Beans* to have its Canadian Thanksgiving holiday on November 1, we shut down the week before for two weeks of rest. When we returned, I'd been told

My TV sons from The New Adventures of Beans Baxter: *Jonathan Ward (left) and Scott Bremner.*

a script was in preparation that would feature Mom, and that I'd dance in it, so I was resting at home and catching up with family things.

I was being lazy and sitting in bed reading at ten in the morning, when the phone rang. It was Savage Steve.

"Hi, how are you?" he asked.

"Great," I said.

"We've been canceled; just now," Steve said.

The only thing I think I said was, "Oh."

We were all in shock because while not a blockbuster, it was a well-liked little show. It was a little uneven, perhaps, but many shows are in their first year. And I was booked on a local morning show the next day to talk about this unique production and what fun we were having.

Of course, I did the show and put a good face on the disappointment. One of the other guests was Joan Embry from the San Diego Zoo with one of their new baby leopards. Having pictures taken after the show and playing with the leopard, Miss Embry kept telling me to be careful. She was right. The leopard bit me on the leg. Nuts.

I can't think of a better place to give you sugar-coated nuts than right here and now.

A visit with Joan Embry and one of her pet cats.

SUGAR-COATED NUTS

1   egg white
1   tablespoon water
1   pound pecans
1   cup sugar
1   teaspoon ground cinnamon
1   teaspoon salt

In a large bowl beat the egg white and the water until stiff and coat the pecans with the mixture. Mix the sugar, cinnamon, and salt together. Coat the nuts with the sugar mixture and place on a cookie sheet. Bake at 250° for 1 hour. Turn the nuts every 15 minutes. Cool and store in a plastic bag. Do not refrigerate.

Makes 1 pound.

Golden Oldies Reunion

In 1983 a whole bunch of us "oldies but goodies" appeared in a TV movie titled *High School, U.S.A.*

An interesting thing happened in that show. There was a young man playing a nice part in the movie as a date of my daughter. He was new, I thought, and awfully good. He had charisma to burn, and I went home and told Harry about him. The young man was Anthony Edwards of *E.R.* fame, and I'm as proud of him as if he were my own.

Dawn Wells, beloved as Mary Ann on *Gilligan's Island,* was also in the movie. She is a delightful person and a great cook. Here's one of her favorite recipes. (You can find this recipe and many more of her delicious recipes in her *Mary Ann's Gilligan's Island Cookbook,* published by Rutledge Hill Press.)

Talk about a high school reunion—how about this TV reunion of actors who starred in shows from the 1950s and 1960s (clockwise from bottom): Dawn Wells, Mary Ann on Gilligan's Island; *Dwayne Hickman, Dobie of* The Many Loves of Dobie Gillis; *David Nelson of* The Adventures of Ozzie and Harriet; *Bob Denver, Gilligan of* Gilligan's Island; *Angela Cartwright of* The Danny Thomas Show *and* Lost in Space; *and me.*

MOM'S MEAT LOAF RAMOO

2 pounds ground chuck
2 teaspoons salt
½ teaspoon pepper
½ teaspoon curry powder
½ teaspoon garlic powder
2 eggs
2 tablespoons minced onion
2 large peeled and chopped Granny Smith apples
½ cup orange juice
⅓ cup chopped chutney

In a large bowl mix together all of the ingredients except the chutney. Line a shallow pan with foil. Shape the mixture into a loaf, place it in the pan, and chill. Bake at 350° for 1 hour.

Remove the meat loaf from the oven and spread with chutney. Return the meat loaf to the oven for 10 minutes.
Serves 6 to 8.

A Lemon of a Winner

Jane Wyatt had gotten me involved with the March of Dimes organization many years before, and in the late 1980s, Harry and I were invited to participate in the Monterey Bay's Gourmet Gala.

I wanted to make something simple so that I could be knowledgeable about it as it was presented, but Jane Wyatt chided me saying, "Anybody can make lemon bars!" She had a good point there, but that was my decision.

Harry and I display our prize-winning lemon squares with violet garnish.

Presenting us our award is Martha Stewart.

Brian, being in the local restaurant scene at that time, acted as our assistant chef, and he and I worked out the presentation and all, and he made the finished product that was tasted by the judges because I didn't have access to our oven.

Some of the judges were terrifyingly famous to us: Craig Claiborne, Jeremiah Tower, and Martha Stewart. We not only won Best Dessert that year, but, wonder of wonders, Best of Show for our simple lemon bars. Thank you, Brian.

LEMON SQUARES

6 tablespoons butter
¼ cup confectioners' sugar
1 cup all-purpose flour
2 eggs
1 cup sugar
2 tablespoons all-purpose flour
2 tablespoons lemon juice
Grated rind of ½ lemon

Preheat the oven to 350°. In a medium bowl blend the butter, confectioners' sugar, and 1 cup of flour. Pat the mixture gently into an 8-inch square pan. Bake for 15 minutes or until golden brown.

Meanwhile, in a separate bowl beat the eggs lightly. In another bowl combine the sugar, 2 tablespoons of flour, the lemon juice, and the lemon rind. Pour this mixture over the hot crust and bake for 15 minutes or until the mixture appears firm.

Sprinkle confectioners' sugar while hot. Loosen the custard top from the edge of the pan while still hot. Cut into squares when cool.

For the Gourmet Gala, each square had a candied violet on it to dress it up.
Makes 20 squares.

Taking It Easy

I was once again a lady of leisure—sort of. No one with a house, pets, a husband, a teenager, and an aging mother is ever truly at leisure. And Share, Inc., voted me second vice president in charge of their second biggest money-maker each year—*The Day by Day Calendar Book.*

Never in my life had I done anything like that and all I could think was—help! I swear, if it hadn't been for Terry Baldwin and Joan Kardashian, I'd have never made it. I owed it all to them.

Harry had had a little cough for a while and decided to see a doctor. That man sent him to another, and that's when we learned he had throat cancer. This was May 1989.

Being a very private person, Harry told no one except the immediate family, and so began an odyssey many others have experienced or will experience in the future. Daily radiation treatments were ordered, and in Harry's case, he suffered severe loss of saliva and the inability to swallow even the softest foods. I became the purée queen. The purée queen of cream. But thanks to God and Dr. Rose at St. Joseph Hospital, Harry beat the cancer and lost only five pounds in the process.

Before long he could eat as before, with no restrictions—except that for the rest of his life he had to drink copious amounts of water.

This has been a family favorite for so long I can't remember, and it was always what Harry craved when he was down (which wasn't often). My mother loved it too, and as I was now taking food to her almost daily, I'd make a lot of this.

CHICKEN FRICASSEE

1   **chicken cut in 10 pieces (save back and wings for other use)**
1   **large onion, cut into 6 to 8 pieces**
3   **to 4 ribs celery, scraped and cut into 2-inch pieces**
3   **to 4 carrots, scraped and cut into 2-inch pieces**
¼   **teaspoon thyme**
    Salt and pepper to taste
1   **10¾-ounce can chicken broth**
½   **cup or more peas, frozen and thawed**
½   **cup cold water, mixed with 2 to 3 tablespoons all-purpose flour**

Wash the chicken in cold running water and place in a Dutch oven. Tuck the onions, celery, and carrots in and around the chicken. Sprinkle on the seasonings. Pour broth over all. Bring up to a boil, cover, and lower heat to simmering. Simmer for 50 minutes to 1 hour.

Remove the chicken pieces to a platter to keep warm. Add the peas to the broth. Make a thickener with the cold water and flour in the lidded container. Shake it up so there are no lumps. Add some hot broth to that and then, quickly whisking as you go, add all of the flour/water mixture to the pot. Simmer, stirring until thickened. Now, bone and skin the chicken breasts and place in the pot. Skin the thighs and legs and place in the pot. Reheat all a wee bit and serve over rice or noodles or with cornbread.

Because I like them and they add richness of flavor, I put the rinsed packet of giblets and neck in to cook with the chicken pieces. Let everyone else have the fancy parts—give me the vegetables and the funny bits any day.
Serves 4 to 6.

At the party for installation of officers of Share, Inc. Harry has newly shaped his beard to accommodate his radiation treatments.

Spring 1990 in Kansas City.

Kansas City, Here I Come

We had a wonderful year (1990) with lots to be grateful for. Chris had been in college and was now on his own singing with a Christian rock band. Harry was well, and I was set to go to Kansas City, Missouri, to work again for two gentlemen whom I'll tell you more about later.

When in Kansas City we had a lot of fun looking at houses and dreaming of retiring and moving away, for we loved that town.

There are two things people think of when they hear Kansas City. One is jazz and the other is barbecue. This is a sauce given me by one of my new friends in the city (more about him later, too), and I hope you enjoy it.

SWEET AND TANGY BARBECUE SAUCE

From Margie Stout, Craig's mother.

1   15-ounce can Hunt's tomato sauce
¼   cup lemon juice
¼   cup vinegar
2   cups brown sugar, loosely packed

Mix together and pour over your meat. Great with brisket, chicken or hamburger. It can be frozen.
Makes about 1 quart.

Another Acting Life

Just as in life, show business is uncertain. You never know what's around the corner.

In the late summer of 1990, I had been at a long Share meeting, had shopped a bit, and then had gotten home about four in the afternoon. I'd planned something for dinner that took a while to prepare and I was looking forward to the process.

The phone rang. It was my agent telling me to go into Hollywood to read for a TV series. I said no and gave him all the excuses, plus this one—I was wearing jeans and no makeup and he wasn't giving me time to change.

"Just go," he demanded, so I went.

And by the next day I was co-starring with Chris Elliott in his new loony series *Get a Life* for Fox Broadcasting.

The show was about the life of a thirty-year-old man who lives with his parents and is a newspaper delivery boy. The premise was so appalling to my son Chris, who had returned to live at home, that when he heard about it that evening, he said, "I'm outta here!"

Within in a month, he had moved out for the last time.

And so began another adventure. Being with all these wonderful people from the end of 1990 until the spring of 1991 meant the world to me. I don't know what I would have done without them.

This is a down-home and comfy dish from the South, courtesy of Ilia Brown, wife of University of Virginia professor Irby Brown.

Would you believe it? We shot Get a Life *at Columbia where I had done* Father Knows Best *thirty years before. It was like coming home.*

CHEESE GRITS CASSEROLE

1	cup grits
4	cups water, salted
½	cup butter
½	roll (3 ounces) Kraft garlic cheese, or 6 tablespoons cheese spread and 1 clove of garlic, pressed
4	slices (4 ounces) processed Swiss cheese
2	eggs beaten
	Whole milk

Cook the grits in salted water according to the directions on the box. While hot, stir in the butter and cheeses. Put the beaten eggs in a measuring cup and fill with whole milk to 1 cup. Fold into the grits. Transfer to a greased casserole dish. Bake at 350° for about 1 hour and 30 minutes.

Let cool (out of the oven). This takes about 10 minutes and this keeps the bottom from being watery.

After all these years, I finally got my own chair!

Bob Elliott of the wonderful duo of Bob and Ray was my TV hubby as we played the parents of wacky Chris Elliott, Bob's real-life son, in Get a Life.

Crossroads

Harry was holding down the fort, nursing a slight cold, while I worked long hours on *Get a Life.* The best part for the actors was that we shot for two weeks and then had one week off.

During one of my off-weeks, I got a phone call. Lou Genevrino, the dancer I'd worked with long ago, had gotten my number from a mutual friend and phoned saying that he'd written a script and he'd like to discuss it with me. Thinking he meant he'd written a role for "moi," I said yes, and we met for coffee.

Actually, he wanted me to get the script to another Share member in hopes of getting it produced. Disappointed, I offered to take it home for Harry to read before anyone else and he agreed.

A few days later, Harry asked for Lou's phone number, saying he liked it, and he'd like to work with the young man on it and see what they could do with it together. I gave Harry the phone number Lou had given me and forgot about the whole thing.

A week later my car just quit in the middle of Hollywood Boulevard and Gower Street during rush hour, and so now, as well as working, I had to think about what kind of car to get.

Harry had always wanted a Cadillac, and so for his November birthday and Christmas and our coming April "Thirtieth Anniversary," we put a down payment on a beautiful powder blue DeVille for him and I took over his station wagon. He was in heaven, like a little boy with his first long pants.

When the license plate arrived, it began with 2UFH. We laughed because it looked like "To you, for Harry!"

Hamming it for the camera on the set of Get a Life *are, left to right, producer David Latt, Chris Elliott, Bob Elliott, me, and writer/producer/director David Mirkin.*

NO-FLOUR CHOCOLATE MERINGUE COOKIES

These cookies are heavenly and light as a cloud.

1   6-ounce package semisweet chocolate chips
2   egg whites (at room temperature)
½   cup (scant)sugar
½   teaspoon vanilla extract or almond extract
1   teaspoon vinegar
     Dash salt
¾   cup chopped nuts or raisins

Preheat the oven to 350°. In a double boiler melt the chocolate chips over hot water. In a large bowl beat the egg whites and salt until foamy. Gradually add the sugar and beat to stiff peaks. Beat in the vanilla and vinegar. Fold in the melted chocolate, and then the nuts or raisins. Drop by the teaspoonful on greased cookie sheets. Bake for about 10 minutes. Cool for a few minutes, and then continue to cool on racks.

Me as Gladys Peterson on Get a Life.

A Sad Time

Harry's cold was dragging him down, but he continued to take the antibiotics the doctor had prescribed. The whole family gathered for the Christmas holidays. We had an unusually simple meal, as the weather was warm, I had been working hard, and Harry just didn't have much appetite.

On New Year's Day, Harry and I went to see a movie and, as he always needed water, he carried a little bottle of it with him wherever we went. As we left the theater, he handed it to me to hold for a minute, and my heart nearly stopped. The bottle was as warm as a cup of tea—just from the heat of Harry's hands. He had quite a fever and had said nothing about it to anyone.

Two days later, while I was at the studio, his son Steve drove him to the doctor's office, where it was discovered that he had a slight pneumonia in both lungs. He was told to rest for two weeks, and he'd be fine.

The next morning he was so sick that I insisted that he let me take him to St. Joseph's on my way to work. With my friend and neighbor Ann Jones's help, we got him into the car and to the hospital, where he was stabilized.

During rehearsal for a scene for *Get a Life* later that morning, David Mirkin handed me a note from the hospital physician asking that I call. I was not alarmed at all because, when I had left Harry that morning, he had his color back, was thanking me for getting him to the emergency room, and was even asking for a newspaper to read.

When I returned the doctor's call after the scene was shot, I found out that Harry had gone into cardiac arrest. His condition was critical and he was hooked up to all sorts of machines. He later slipped into a coma.

I cannot and shall not share with you the next three weeks. I'm sure you can imagine what it was like. The family was there in shifts and I spent most nights on a sofa in the lounge of the intensive care unit.

Everyone on the set of *Get a Life* was wonderful to me. As we were coming to the end of a set of shows, David Mirkin asked me—no matter what—to do my last two scenes so that we could

Plucking fruit from our orange tree.

stay on schedule. I heartily agreed, for, after three weeks, I didn't see any major changes coming in Harry's condition.

But that night the doctors and our family made the decision to turn off the machines. Early Sunday, while I was holding his hand and saying "The Lord's Prayer," Harry peacefully left this life. My best friend was gone.

And I kept my promise to the cast and crew of *Get a Life.* With my head held high, I was on the set at 6:00 A.M. Monday to shoot my last two scenes. They were the most difficult few hours of my life.

Harry had been very proud of our citrus trees (all both of them), but he got a kick out of the lemon one because it would just keep cranking out fruit like a machine—hence, all these lemon recipes. So, on the saying "when life gives you lemons, make lemonade," I'll give you Harry's most favorite lemon dessert. It was also a favorite of composer John Williams.

LEMON DESSERT

3   **eggs, separated**
    Sugar
1   **lemon**
½   **pint whipping cream**
    Vanilla wafers

You'll need 3 bowls. In a large bowl beat the egg whites and then add 3 tablespoons of sugar. In a medium bowl beat the egg yolks and add 1 cup of sugar plus the juice of one lemon and the grated rind of the same lemon (grate it before juicing; it saves the skin on the fingers). In a large bowl whip the cream and add all together and place in an ice cube tray. I line mine with foil. Crush vanilla wafers on top.

Place in the freezer compartment for several hours or, better, overnight. Serve in your prettiest dessert cups or stemmed glasses with good cookies.
Serves 4.

Show Stopper

This time also proved to be nearly the end of *Get a Life.* A new format was planned for the 1991-92 season because Chris's real dad, Bob Elliott, did not wish to continue, and so we three shot a few scenes to be inserted in future shows and that was that.

But as hard as this period was, unbeknownst to me, a rainbow was on the horizon. Peter and Marie were expecting their first child. Also, on a rainy Sunday a month or more after Harry's death, I made a pot of chili. After taking some to Mother, I still had a lot left.

I was terribly lonely, but I didn't want family and I didn't want neighbors. I wanted to be around some people or someone who barely knew me, and I wanted to feed them. I don't know why. So I called Lou Genevrino. As it happened, he was at his family home back East at the time, but when he returned a month later, he called and we began having coffee and church "dates."

Lou would stop by with his Bible and we'd visit and talk. And he made me laugh for the first time in many months. By the end of the summer, we knew were in love and would marry.

By the Christmas of 1991, I was a grandmother for the first time, and Lou and I were planning a wedding for 1992! All the boys were happy at the outcome, and my Mother—wonder of wonders—adored Lou from the first time she met him.

Lou, who has been a devout Catholic since birth, brought that peace and joy into my heart and life. Let me share this with you in honor of all of the wonderful priests and people I've met at St. Charles Borromeo Parish in North Hollywood.

The cast and crew of Get a Life. *Betcha didn't know it took that many people to put on a TV series, did you?*

MONASTERY PUMPKIN BREAD

3½ cups sifted all-purpose flour
3   cups sugar
2   teaspoons baking soda
1   teaspoon ground cinnamon
1   teaspoon ground nutmeg
1½ teaspoons salt
4   eggs, beaten
1   cup oil
⅔   cup water
2   cups cooked and mashed pumpkin
    Walnut pieces

Preheat the oven to 350°. In a large bowl stir together the flour, sugar, baking soda, cinnamon, nutmeg, and salt. Combine the eggs, oil, water, and pumpkin, mixing well. Stir the pumpkin mixture into the dry ingredients. Turn into 3 greased 5 x 9-inch loaf pans and top with several walnut pieces. Bake for 1 hour or a until cake tester inserted in the center comes out clean. Cool before slicing. This bread freezes well and tastes best slightly warm and buttered.
Makes 3 1-pound loaves.

A New Direction

Wedding Day

I was finally to have a real church wedding. It was everything I'd ever hoped and dreamed it might be. The cake, the flowers, everything!

The children came from all over. Brian and Nancy from Monterey, Sue and her husband and three children from Sacramento, and James and Martha from New York. Stephen took the photos and the others were there to share in the joy of the day.

This is a terrific brunch dish from the wife of one of Lou's dearest friends, Vickie Minkoff, and would be perfect for a wedding shower or for any occasion.

The newlyweds.

VICKIE'S BRUNCH EGGS

2	tablespoons butter
1	small onion, finely chopped
2	cups frozen corn
1	dozen eggs
1½	cups sour cream
½	cup milk
4	cups Cheddar cheese, shredded
1	8-ounce can diced chilies
1	tablespoon Worcestershire sauce
1	teaspoon salt
1	teaspoon pepper

In a skillet melt the butter and sauté the onion until soft. Add the corn for a few minutes and set aside. Beat the eggs and add the remaining ingredients, including the onion and corn. Pour into a buttered oblong pan. Bake at 325° for 1 hour and 15 minutes.

Serve with sour cream, salsa, and guacamole.

Serves 8.

Brian asked Lou if he could call him "Dad," and Lou said sure. Brian then said, "Can I borrow $5?"

Stephen Ackerman when young.

Kids Cook the Most Delicious Things

Now I want to give you the children's favorites from their own homes.

The first is from the home of Francine and Steve. His barbecued turkey is in an earlier chapter, and this is a soup that his wife, a busy career woman, can make on the weekends.

DUMPLING SOUP

1   cup olive oil
5   tablespoons all-purpose flour
4   medium size yellow onions (cut in
      half, then in quarters)
2   46-ounce cans of V-8 juice
1   46-ounce can water
5   parsnips (cut in $\frac{1}{2}$-inch rounds)
5   ribs celery
2   teaspoons sugar
4   eggs
      Salt and pepper
      Parsley ($\frac{1}{2}$ of bunch chopped up)

In a large soup pot heat the olive oil and
then mix in the flour until smooth. Add the
onions. Sauté until soft and add the V-8 juice
and water. Boil slowly and then mix thoroughly over heat for 30 minutes.

Add the parsnips, celery, parsley, and
salt and pepper to taste. Simmer for 30 minutes.

Dumplings:
4   eggs
      Salt to taste
6   tablespoons all-purpose flour

In a large bowl beat the eggs very well (until
they are very light) and then add the salt
and flour to form a smooth dough with no
lumps. In another, larger pot boil water.
Scoop in a tablespoon of the dough. It will
sink and when done will float. Continue
with the remaining dough. When all the
dumplings are cooked, transfer to the soup
without any water on them. Serve hot.

The Stephen Ackerman family: Stephen, Francine, Jessica, left, and Daley.

Having a Ball

Yes, folks, there really is a Susan Ackerman Peterson. She's like the Phantom when it comes to photos, but she has given me so much love through the years that her presence is felt without pictures.

Now, she is famous for her cheese ball. Her husband Richard and she are avid Nebraska Cornhusker football fans, and she always serves this at her TV parties while watching the games.

Susan and brother Stephen.

Susan in high school.

SUSAN'S FAMOUS CORN-HUSKERS CHEESE BALL

2   8-ounce packages cream cheese (may substitute light cheese)
½   pound New York sharp cheese, grated (no substitutions)
1   medium onion, grated
    Dash salt
¼   teaspoon celery salt
2   tablespoons Worcestershire sauce
    Chopped walnuts

In a medium bowl mix all of ingredients except for the walnuts. Form in a ball and place in the freezer for about 10 minutes.

Roll in the chopped nuts and serve with crackers.
Serves 6 to 8.

Susan and Richard's children, when young: son Brett and twins Carey and Kelly.

Brian, a budding chef and sailor, at age eight.

Inventive Chef

Brian's recipes are of his very own devising. He's a talented cook and now that he doesn't have to do it for a living, I suspect he enjoys it even more. He knows how I love salmon and spinach, so he came up with these delicious dishes.

CRUSTY BAKED SALMON WITH LEMON-SHALLOT BEURRE BLANC

2   **pounds of fresh salmon filet, skinned**
1   **cup seasoned bread crumbs**

Lemon-Shallot Beurre Blanc:
⅓   **cup sliced shallot**
¼   **cup cold butter, cut into slices**
2   **tablespoons lemon juice**
      Zest of 1 lemon
⅓   **cup dry white wine**
1   **tablespoon chopped parsley**

Preheat the oven to 375°. With a pair of tweezers or small needle-nosed pliers, gently pull the pin bones from the filet. Cut the filet into 4 equal portions, dredge in the bread crumbs and place in a shallow, lightly-greased baking dish. Place in the oven and bake for about 30 minutes.

Just before the salmon is done, sauté the shallot with 1 teaspoon of the butter. When the shallot is clear and translucent but before the butter begins to brown, add the wine and lemon juice and lemon zest. Simmer until the liquid reduces. Place the salmon portions on plates. When most but not all of the liquid has reduced, add the remaining slices of butter. With a gentle, swirling motion in the pan (do not stir), incorporate the melting butter into the shallot-liquid mixture. As soon as the rest of the butter has melted, add the chopped parsley, and then spoon over the salmon.

Accompany with rice pilaf and Creamed Spinach Ackerman.
Serves 4.

CREAMED SPINACH ACKERMAN

3   **bunches fresh spinach**
1   **tablespoon olive oil**
¼   **cup minced shallot**
2   **garlic cloves, minced**
¼   **cup dry vermouth**
1   **teaspoon caraway seeds**
½   **cup heavy cream**
½   **cup grated Parmesan cheese**
      Salt and pepper to taste

Thoroughly wash the spinach and remove the stems. Drain and set aside. In a deep saucepan sauté the shallot and garlic in very hot olive oil. Add the vermouth (carefully, or it will flambé). After the alcohol has burned off, allow to reduce until most of the liquid is gone. Add the cream and bring to a boil.

Chiffonade the spinach (cut into thin strips) and add to the cream mixture. Stir in the caraway and the cheese. Continue stirring until all of the spinach has incorporated and the cheese has melted. Reduce to a low simmer. Add salt and pepper to taste. Popeye would be proud.

More Family Favorites

Peter, Marie, and their two beautiful children, Harry III and Amy, live close to us in the San Fernando Valley. Peter, as I mentioned earlier, is not a cook, but Marie more than makes up for it.

Peter and Marie's little ones, Harry III and Amy.

THE GRANDMA SPECIAL
(Grilled Peanut Butter
and Jelly Sandwich)

"This was made for me by Nana when I would be homesick and she needed to take care of me. This is also especially good on a cold and rainy day."—Peter

2   slices white bread
    Butter or margarine (stick or spread)
    Peanut butter (smooth is best)
    Jelly or preserves (grape or strawberry)

Make a peanut butter and jelly sandwich on white bread. Spread butter or margarine onto one side of the sandwich. Preheat the skillet for a minute and put the buttered side of the bread slices onto the skillet. While that is cooking, butter the other side of the sandwich (the one that faces up in the skillet). Turn the sandwich over when the one side is grilled and grill the other side. When complete cut diagonally and serve on a plate. A hot bowl of Ramen noodle soup goes well with this.
Serves 1.

MARIE'S PASTA

I serve this dish often because it is fast and easy. I don't usually add sausage, but every once in a while I crave my favorite sausage, and it makes the dish even more yummy.—Marie

8   to 16 ounces of angel hair, spaghetti, or your favorite pasta
¾   to 1 pound of Adeli's fresh turkey with sun-dried tomato Sausage (optional)
¼   cup olive oil
½   cup chopped onion
2   medium-sized zucchini, halved and sliced
2   cloves garlic, minced
2   15-ounce cans diced tomatoes
1½ tablespoons fresh chopped basil or crushed dried basil
Salt to taste (optional)
Parmesan cheese, grated

In a large pot cook the pasta according to the package instructions. Meanwhile in a skillet cook the turkey (and sausage) until done. Drain off any fat. Remove from the pan. Put the olive oil in the pan over medium heat. Add the onion when the oil is hot. Cook the onion until tender. Add the zucchini and stir until all pieces are coated with oil. Cook until tender, about 3 minutes. Add the garlic and cook for 1 minute. Add the cans of tomatoes with juice. Add the basil and sausage and cook for about 5 minutes, stirring frequently.

Pour the sauce over the pasta on plates. Top with cheese. A nice bottle of merlot goes with this dish.
Serves 4 to 6.

Recipe from the Old Country

James and Martha live in London, England, with their two children, Holden and Lily. Martha is a full-time homemaker after many years of fashion modeling, and James is currently an executive with British Sky Broadcasting.

This is one of Martha's recipes that she wants to share with you.

James and Martha's wedding.

VEAL CHOPS WITH ARUGULA AND BALSAMIC VINEGAR

1 large egg
½ cup milk
1½ cups bread crumbs
  Salt and pepper
4 large veal chops with bone pounded
   relatively thin
1 large bunch of arugula
2 to 3 large ripe good quality tomatoes
  Olive oil
  Very good quality balsamic vinegar
   (very aged is best)

In a shallow dish beat the egg and milk together. Season the bread crumbs with salt and pepper. Dip the veal chops in the egg mixture to coat and then into bread crumbs. Meanwhile chop the arugula and tomatoes into medium-size chunks and set aside separately. Sauté the veal chops in olive oil for about 3 minutes per side. Remove and drain on paper towels. Top with a large handful of arugula and a handful of tomatoes. Pour about 1 to 2 teaspoons of balsamic vinegar on top and a couple of tablespoons of olive oil. Serve immediately.

Christmas 1997 in Apple Valley with Chris and Leeann.

More Wedding Bells

Chris and LeeAnn are the newlyweds in the family, and because they both work (he does computer graphics and she has her own nail salon business), they haven't any recipes of their own.

Leeann's mom, Joan Landry, is a superb cook and, as the matriarch of a huge family, has to do lots of it. Here are a couple of her favorites.

SPEEDY STROGANOFF LOAF

1½ pounds ground beef
½ cup chopped onion
1 cup water
½ cup dairy sour cream
¼ cup sliced ripe olives
1 envelope stroganoff seasoning mix
1 loaf French bread
   Green pepper slices
   Cherry tomatoes
   Shredded Cheddar cheese

In a large skillet, cook the beef and onion until browned, and then drain off any excess fat. Stir in the water, sour cream, olives, and seasoning mix. Cover and simmer for 10 minutes. Cut the bread in half, lengthwise. Toast under the broiler until brown, spread with butter. Spread half the meat mixture on each half of bread. Arrange the green pepper slices alternately with the cherry tomato halves and sprinkle with cheese. Place on a baking sheet. Bake at 375° for 7 to 10 minutes.
Serves 6.

CHOCOLATE SHEET CAKE

2 cups sugar
2 cups all-purpose flour
½ cup shortening
1 stick butter
4 tablespoons cocoa
1 cup water
2 eggs, slightly beaten
½ cup milk
1 tablespoon baking soda
1 teaspoon ground cinnamon
1 teaspoon vanilla extract

Preheat the oven to 400°. In a large bowl combine the sugar and flour.

In a saucepan combine and melt together the shortening, butter, cocoa, and water. Bring to a boil.

Add the melted ingredients to the sugar and flour. Add the eggs, milk, baking soda, cinnamon, and vanilla. The batter will be thin.

Pour into a lightly greased 11 x 16-inch pan. Bake for 25 minutes.

Start making the icing 5 minutes before the cake is done and ice the cake immediately after removing from the oven.

Icing:
½ cup butter
6 tablespoons milk
4 tablespoons cocoa
1 teaspoon vanilla extract
1 16-ounce box confectioners' sugar
1 cup nuts (optional)

In a saucepan combine the buttter, milk, and cocoa, and bring to a boil. Remove from the heat and add the vanilla, confectioners' sugar, and nuts. Spread on the cake.

This has been a family favorite for twenty-seven years. We have fourteen birthdays a year in our family, and this cake is always requested.
Serves 8.

My own crew of bodyguards at Chris and Leann's wedding are (left to right) Peter, Brian, Chris, James, and Steve. And aren't they handsome devils?

Where The Feet Meet The Floor

Lou, who is now a licensed hardwood flooring contractor, had a fine career as a dancer on Broadway and in road companies of such hits as *Do Re Mi, Fiddler on the Roof* (he was an original bottle dancer), *Fiorello* with Tom Bosley, *Westside Story,* and *Sugar.* He later appeared in the Las Vegas acts of Tina Sinatra and Ann-Margret and with Donald O'Connor in *Little Me.*

He is a full-blooded Italian, and his mother let me have her family recipe for sauce as a wedding present.

Lou and me.

THE GENEVRINO FAMILY SAUCE

3   to 5 tablespoons best olive oil
3   large cans Italian tomatoes with basil
2   cloves garlic, left whole
3   teaspoons dried basil
1½ teaspoons dried oregano
¾   teaspoon dried mint
¼   teaspoon (or less) dried red pepper
3   tablespoons Italian (flat leaf) parsley,
    minced (this is fresh parsley and I
    am not stingy with the tablespoons)

In a blender purée the canned tomatoes, then pour into a food mill that is set over a bowl. Drain and press out all but the seeds. No seeds should be in the sauce. In a large iron skillet or heavy non-stick one heat the olive oil and whole garlic cloves. Do not brown or the garlic will make the sauce bitter. Add the strained tomatoes and all seasonings; stir and bring up the heat to a high simmer, and then lower the heat. Cook, occasionally stirring the bottom and sides of the pan, for 2 to 3 hours or until very thick. It reduces by nearly half, so make plenty. I try to make 2 batches at a time in 2 skillets, then freeze for later. This is the greatest!

Note: The first time I made this, the stovetop looked like the scene of the St. Valentine's Day Massacre. Just wipe it with a damp cloth when you're finished and all will be well.

Grace and Speed

After our marriage, I chose to become a Catholic. We attend St. Charles Borromeo in North Hollywood, where Lou is a Sacristan and I am a Lector. We've made many new friends there and often gather after morning Mass for breakfast.

One couple is Ernie and Gini Rodriguez. She is a homemaker and he, with his sons and grandsons, build and race Formula Mazda cars all over the United States.

Here is one of their family favorites.

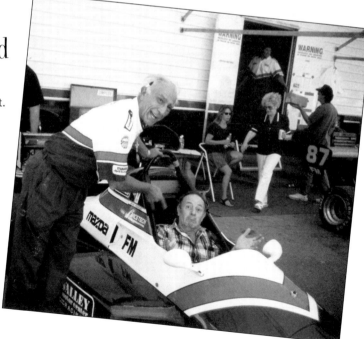

Ernie helps Lou get ready for the big race in Ernie's car. Gini is in the background walking toward the car. No doubt, to stop the horsing around!

TAMALE PIE

2	cloves garlic
1	cup chopped onion
4	tablespoons oil
1	pound ground beef
1	20-ounce can cream corn
1	28-ounce can tomatoes
4	tablespoons chili powder
4	teaspoons salt
2	cups yellow cornmeal
2	12-ounce cans tomato juice
2	cans black olives
1	cup shredded Cheddar cheese

In a skillet heat the oil and cook the garlic and onion until soft. Brown the beef. In a large pan combine the corn, tomatoes, and seasoning. Add the garlic, onion, and browned beef. Simmer for 20 minutes. Add the cornmeal a little at a time with the tomato juice. It'll be very thick. Stir constantly. Add the olives but save some for the top. Pour in a casserole and top with shredded cheese and the rest of the olives. Bake at 350° for 30 minutes.
Serves 4 to 6.

Lou downs a cup of java and dreams of Eggplant Parmesan.

Egging Me On

As of this writing, Lou and I have been married six years, and one hot summer day a few years ago I decided to make Eggplant Parmesan. Lou's mother's version was the only one that he would eat, and she had just given me the recipe. I had plenty of sauce from the freezer and nothing much to do that day, so I thought I would give it a try.

Mother G's secret was to slice the eggplant very thin and to drain it very well on paper towels after cooking and before assembling the dish. My kitchen is not very large, and I had eggplant from one end of it to the other, and as we have no air conditioning, it got very hot in there with all the frying and draining. And there was every likelihood that it still wouldn't taste like his mother's.

To make a long story short, it passed the test with flying colors, and now you can make it, too.

MRS. G.'S EGGPLANT PARMESAN

1   medium eggplant, peeled and sliced
       very thin
2   eggs and a bit of milk for an egg wash
      Small bit of olive oil
      Sauce
      Grated mozzarella cheese
      Grated Parmesan cheese (I prefer
        Regiano)

Dip the eggplant in the egg-wash and fry quickly in a small bit of oil (more can be added if needed as you go) on high heat. Drain pieces on paper towels and continue until all is cooked.

Brush a baking pan (9 x 13-inch glass is what I use) with a small bit of olive oil and layer the eggplant, sauce, mozzarella, and Parmesan until you have used up the eggplant, probably three layers. This all depends on how many you'll want to serve, the size of the eggplant, the size of your baking pan, etc. This can't be exact, just have fun with it and reap your compliments.

Bake at 350° for 30 minutes or until the cheeses are melted and it is well heated throughout.

Share Fare

The current president of Share, Inc., is Patricia Bosley, wife of stage and TV star Tom Bosley, well-remembered as Ron Howard's dad Mr. Cunningham on *Happy Days* and as the priest who solved crimes on *Father Dowling Mysteries.* Patricia is a cheerful, positive-thinking woman who has led Share well in many capacities these past few years. And I'm pleased that she agreed to "share" this with you.

Patricia and Tom Bosley.

FETTUCINE ALFREDO

1   tablespoon margarine
2   small garlic cloves, minced
1   tablespoon all-purpose flour
1⅓ cups skim milk
2   tablespoons light cream cheese
1¼ cups freshly grated Parmesan cheese, divided
4   cups hot cooked fettucine
2   teaspoons chopped fresh parsley
    Pepper

In a skillet melt the margarine and sauté the garlic in the margarine for 1 minute. Stir in the flour. Gradually add the milk, stirring constantly until it thickens. Add the cream cheese and 2 minutes later add 1 cup of the Parmesan cheese; stir until it melts. Pour over the hot fettucine. Top with the remaining cheese and parsley. Season with pepper to taste.
Serves 3 to 4.

Actress Jane Greer Lasker

Share and Share Alike

Through all my years in Share, I've made many friends. They have been there through thick and thin, and I'm so grateful to have had the opportunity to know them and be a part of this wonderful organization and all the good they do for others less fortunate than themselves.

There are too many names to mention, but one whom I asked to send a recipe wanted you to have this one. She is Jane Greer Lasker, who is now retired from her motion picture and television career of many years. She starred in films with Robert Mitchum, Kirk Douglas, Trevor Howard, Richard Widmark, and many others. Many film noire fans consider her 1947 film *Out of the Past,* with Mitchum and Douglas, the best of its genre.

Jane and her companion Frank London, an actor and drama coach, devised this recipe just for you.

DIJON HONEY CHICKEN

1   5-pound chicken, chicken neck,
       giblets and liver
2   cloves garlic, crushed
1   spring fresh rosemary
3   tablespoons Dijon mustard
3   tablespoons honey
     Sprinkle garlic powder
     Water for basting

Preheat the oven to 375°. Rub crushed garlic into the cavity with a brush or your fingers. Add the fresh rosemary, neck, giblets, and liver to the cavity. Place the chicken breast side down on a rack and place the rack in a pan (with water in the bottom) into the oven. Baste every 20 minutes for 1 hour.

Then turn the chicken breast side up until browned, about 15 to 20 minutes. Turn off the oven.

Combine the Dijon and honey, and spread the mixture over the chicken. Add the garlic powder and remove from the oven.
Serves 4 to 6.

Jane Greer in a publicity shot taken around 1960.

Special Times to Share

One of my newest friends in Share is Annie Gaybis Byner. She is married to comedian John Byner, and they, too, have been married only a short while.

Lou and I have had the pleasure of their company in San Diego and Palm Springs, as well as Las Vegas, and an hilarious and enjoyable time it always is.

They are vegetarians, though they'll eat fish on occasion. And so I offer this on their behalf.

It was given to me years ago by comedy writer Peggy Chantler Dick. Her husband is former actor, now psychotherapist, Dr. Douglas Dick. He co-starred in one of my favorite Hitchcock movies, *Rope*.

Here is what I call "The Tomato Thing"—a great side dish with chicken, fish, or beef, or with an all-vegetarian meal.

THE TOMATO THING

2   pints cherry tomatoes
    Boiling water
½   cup olive oil
2   tablespoons red wine vinegar
2   cloves garlic, finely minced
    Salt and freshly ground black pepper
      to taste
1   tablespoon chopped parsley

Cover the tomatoes with boiling water and let stand 10 to 15 seconds. (Note: If you let them stand a bit too long, they get kind of squishy. They should be firm.)

Drain the tomatoes quickly. When the tomatoes are cool enough to handle, peel by pulling the skin away with a paring knife. It should come off easily.

Combine the remaining ingredients and pour over the tomatoes. Chill at least 1 hour before serving.

Annie Gaybis and John Byner enjoy a day at the DelMar Race Track in San Diego.

Civic Pride

Anne Jeffreys Sterling is a member of Share, Inc., and she is so much more. She has balanced a successful career with family life and has devoted her spare moments to important civic and fund-raising duties in Los Angeles. She is, as well, one of the most beautiful women I've ever met and she's a great cook. Hey, I think I'm jealous!

Anne Jeffreys Sterling.

STERLING TOFFEE BARS

1   cup butter
1   cup firmly packed brown sugar
1   egg yolk
1   teaspoon vanilla extract
1   cup all-purpose flour
¼   teaspoon salt
1   7-ounce milk chocolate bar, broken
      into small pieces
½   cup toasted slivered almonds

Beat the butter and brown sugar until light and creamy. Add the egg yolk, vanilla, flour, and salt and mix. Spread in a buttered 9 x 13-inch baking pan, and bake at 350° until brown, about 20 minutes. The batter will rise and fall slightly. Remove from the oven and immediately sprinkle with chocolate pieces. Then spread the chocolate evenly as it melts. Top immediately with almonds, and let cool completely. Cut into squares and store in an airtight container.
Makes about 24 squares.

Dennis Hennessy, left, and Richard Carruthers.

Entrées Take Center Stage

Over the years I've had the pleasure of working for Richard Carruthers and Dennis Hennessy in Kansas City, Kansas and Missouri, three times—the latest in November 1996 to February 1997 in the play *Never Too Late.*

They are the most wonderful people to work for and their whole organization is run so well that it is no surprise that their New Theatre Restaurant in Overland Park is such a resounding success.

Here are two favorites of the patrons of their dinner theater and I'm sure they will be yours as well.

BOURBON PASTA

Dennis D. Hennessy/The New Theatre Restaurant

2   quarts heavy cream
1   quart chicken stock
12 ounces good bourbon whiskey
1   cup Swiss cheese, shredded
1   cup Fontina cheese, shredded
1   tablespoon fresh garlic, minced
1   tablespoon kosher salt
2   teaspoons cracked black pepper

1   cantaloupe, peeled and diced
1   honeydew melon, peeled and diced
4   ounces lemon juice
1   teaspoon kosher salt

2   pounds dry pasta (Pick a shape, a bite-sized one that holds sauce, like penne, is best)
1   bunch fresh parsley, chopped, for liberal garnishing

In a heavy saucepan combine the cream, chicken stock, bourbon, Swiss cheese, Fontina cheese, garlic, salt, and pepper. Reduce by half. When the sauces like this are cooked over slow heat, the liquids with the least viscosity evaporate first. The bourbon and the water contained in all of liquids will cook away and thicken the sauce while intensifying the flavors.

Toss the fruit in a stainless bowl with the salt and lemon juice. Chill for 1 hour.

Cook the pasta until it's al dente. Drain, rinse with hot water to remove excess starch, toss with olive oil, and hold hot.

Drain the juices from the fruit. Combine the hot sauce, fruit, and pasta in a mixing bowl; add salt and pepper to taste. Plate it up. Garnish with fresh parsley.
Serves 12.

CHICKEN SATE WITH PEANUT SAUCE

Richard Carruthers/The New Theatre Restaurant

Marinade:

1	tablespoon light brown sugar
1	tablespoon curry powder
2	tablespoons crunchy peanut butter
½	cup soy sauce
½	cup freshly squeezed lime juice
2	garlic cloves, minced
	Dried chili pepper, crushed
6	boneless chicken breast halves, skinned, cut into ½-inch wide strips

Peanut sauce:

⅔	cup crunchy peanut butter
1½	cups unsweetened coconut milk
¼	cup freshly squeezed lemon juice
2	tablespoon soy sauce
2	tablespoons molasses (or brown sugar)
1	teaspoon fresh ginger root, grated
4	garlic cloves, minced
¼	cup chicken broth
¼	cup heavy cream
	Cayenne pepper
	Lime zest, grated
	Fresh cilantro sprigs

To make the marinade, combine the first 7 ingredients in a shallow dish. Thread the chicken strips onto bamboo skewers in a serpentine fashion. Place the skewers into the soy sauce mixture and let marinate in the refrigerator for at least 2 hours, although overnight is preferable.

Make the peanut sauce by combining the first 7 sauce ingredients (peanut butter through garlic) in a saucepan. Season to taste with cayenne pepper. Cook over moderate heat, stirring constantly, until the sauce is as thick as heavy cream (about 15 minutes). Transfer to a food processor or blender and purée briefly. Add chicken broth and cream and blend until smooth. This mixture can be made several hours ahead and stored in the refrigerator. Bring to room temperature before serving.

Prepare moderate-hot charcoal coals or preheat a broiler. Cook the skewered chicken, turning several times and basting with the marinade, until crispy on the outside but still moist on the inside, about 8 minutes. Sprinkle the grilled chicken with lime zest and garnish with cilantro leaves. Serve with the peanut sauce for dipping.
Serves 9.

The interior of the New Theatre Restaurant in Overland Park, Kansas.

Kansas City Star

Jeannine Hutchings played my best friend in *Never Too Late,* and life imitated art. We became good friends and chatter on the phone from time to time or over lunch when I'm lucky enough to be in Kansas City.

   She is a talented actress who does it all—films, television, and theater. And, if this recipe is any indication, she is as talented in the kitchen, too.

My good friend Jeannine Hutchings of Kansas City.
Photograph by James M. Goss.

HERBED ROLLS

1	package yeast
3	tablespoons warm water
½	cup butter-flavored shortening
1	teaspoon salt
1	cup hot water
2	eggs, beaten
½	cup sugar
4	cups all-purpose flour

Filling:

⅓	to ½ cup butter or margarine, softened
2	to 4 tablespoons chopped fresh basil (or 2 to 4 teaspoons dried)
2	tablespoons dried parsley flakes
2	teaspoons garlic powder
2	teaspoons chopped fresh chives

Combine the yeast and warm water and set aside. Combine the shortening and salt in hot water and let stand until lukewarm. In a large bowl combine the eggs with sugar and then add the yeast and shortening mixtures. Stir in 2 cups of the flour and beat well with spoon, and then add the remaining flour gradually. Place in a bowl, cover and put in the refrigerator overnight.

About 1 hour and 30 minutes to 2 hours before serving, divide and roll the dough into four circles about ¼-inch thick. Combine the filling ingredients and spread on the dough. Cut into pie-shaped wedges and roll, starting at the larger end. Let the dough rise on greased cookie sheets in a warm (200°) oven until raised. Heat the oven to 400° and bake for about 6 minutes. *Makes 40 to 48 rolls.*

Kansas City Son

Craig Benton played Charlie, the son-in-law in *Never Too Late.* He is as delightful a person as he is an actor. He and his darling wife, Kris, sent lots of recipes to choose from, so I chose these.

Craig Benton.

SCALLOPED CORN

2   15-ounce cans cream style corn
2   eggs
⅓   cup milk
4   tablespoons all-purpose flour
4   tablespoons sugar
1   teaspoon salt
     Butter
     Bread crumbs

In a large bowl combine the corn, eggs, milk, flour, sugar, and salt. Pour into an 8-inch square pan. Dot with butter and cover with bread crumbs. Bake uncovered at 350° for 1 hour.
Serves 4 to 6.

The playbill cover from Never Too Late.

CHEESY CHICKEN BAKE

2   chicken breasts (halved and boned)
1   10¾-ounce can cream of celery soup
1   10¾-ounce can cream of chicken soup
½   cup cooking sherry
6   ounces grated Cheddar cheese
     Paprika
1   package slivered almonds

Place the chicken breasts in a 9 x 13-inch pan. Mix the soups and sherry together and pour over the chicken. Sprinkle cheese over the top, along with the paprika and almonds. Bake at 275° for 2½ to 3 hours.

This is particularly good served over egg noodles or rice with broccoli served on the side.
Serves 4.

Farr Fare

Jamie Farr recently made a second appearance at the New Theatre Restaurant in a production of *George Washington Slept Here,* and I know it won't be his last, as the audiences are just wild about him.

He loves eggplant in many ways but doesn't care for spicy recipes. He and his wife, Joy, gave me carte blanche on this, so here goes.

Jamie Farr.

LEBANESE EGGPLANT DIP

1	large eggplant
¼	cup tahini (sesame seed paste)
1	clove garlic, pressed
2	tablespoons lemon juice
2	tablespoons olive oil
	Salt to taste
	Chopped fresh parsley for garnish

In a 400° oven bake the eggplant until tender, about 40 minutes. Peel the cooled eggplant and mash with a fork. Add the next 4 ingredients and salt to taste. Cover the bowl and store in a refrigerator until needed. Before serving, stir thoroughly and transfer to a serving bowl and garnish with parsley. Serve at room temperature with pita bread or fresh vegetables.

A Caring Place

Currently, as well as working from time to time, I volunteer at Providence St. Joseph Medical Center. All my sons were born there and that is where Harry received his successful cancer treatments and where his life ended later on.

The gals I work with are fun and wise and we share our life stories—and recipes—with each other as time permits. These are two that came my way from Jan Shurke and Helen Henderson.

Helen L. Henderson.

HELEN'S APRICOT COFFEE CAKE

½   cup firmly packed brown sugar
2   tablespoons margarine
2   tablespoons grated orange rind
1   16-ounce can apricot halves, drained
1   10-count package refrigerator biscuits

Preheat the oven to 425°. Grease an 8-inch round cake pan and set aside. In a large mixing bowl, combine the brown sugar, margarine, and orange rind. Arrange the apricots cut side down in the greased pan. Sprinkle with brown sugar mixture. Arrange the biscuits over the brown sugar mixture. Bake in a 425° oven for 8 to 12 minutes. Remove from the oven and let stand for a few minutes. Invert the pan on a large plate and allow the coffee cake to cool slightly before lifting the pan.
Serves 6.

KRISPIE COOKIES

3½ cups all-purpose flour
1   teaspoon salt
1   teaspoon soda
1   teaspoon cream of tartar

1   cup sugar
1   cup brown sugar
1   cup oil
1   cup margarine
1   egg

1   teaspoon vanilla extract
1   teaspoon quick oats
1   cup Rice Krispies
1   cup coconut
½   cup chopped pecans (or walnuts)

Preheat the oven to 350°. Sift the flour, salt, soda, and cream of tartar. In a large mixing bowl, cream the sugars, oil, margarine, and egg. Combine with the flour mixture. Then add the vanilla, oats, Rice Krispies, coconut, and nuts. Roll into balls. Press down with a glass and bake on an ungreased cookie sheet for 12 to 15 minutes.

Jan Shurke and I do volunteer work together at Providence St. Joseph Medical Center. Behind the camera is our best buddy, volunteer Barbara Olson. The photographer never gets in the picture!

Westward Ho!

In 1994, happiness came around the corner by surprise in the form of Beth Sullivan and *Dr. Quinn, Medicine Woman.* I was called to play Rebecca, Dr. Quinn's eldest sister. Of course, Dr. Quinn is so beautifully portrayed by Jane Seymour.

Each year I've been privileged to take part in two episodes of epic proportion—illness, marriage, birth, and death—and have thoroughly enjoyed myself.

Ms. Sullivan and her husband Jim Knobeloch, who plays Jake Slicker, are a loving couple who, during Dr. Quinn's baby boom a few years ago, made their contribution in the form of adorable twins, a boy and a girl.

Jane Seymour and actor/director husband James Keach had twin boys near the same time, and Jane's makeup woman, Lisa Nielsen, had a boy. (Just one.)

This is one bunch of busy parents, and this recipe that Beth Sullivan shares reflects the need and desire to plan ahead to make life a little easier. Here is her delicious Basil Breakfast Strata.

My favorite picture of myself on the set of Dr. Quinn *with Jim Knobeloch in character as Jake Slicker.*

BASIL BREAKFAST STRATA

1   cup milk
½   cup dry white wine
1   day-old loaf French bread, cut into
        ½-inch slices
2   cups arugula leaves (1 bunch)
3   tablespoons olive oil
1   pound basil torta cheese, thinly sliced
        (you can also use basil torta with
        sun-dried tomatoes)
1   ripe tomato, sliced
½   cup pesto
4   or 5 eggs, beaten (depending on what
        thickness you want)
     Salt and freshly ground pepper to
        taste
½   cup heavy cream

One day before serving, mix the milk and wine in shallow bowl. Dip the bread in the mixture, gently squeezing as much liquid as possible from the bread without tearing it.

Place one layer of bread in a 12-inch round oval or round au gratin dish and cover with a layer of arugula leaves dipped in oil, a layer of slices of basil torta, and a layer of tomatoes. Drizzle sparingly with pesto. Repeat the layering until the dish is filled (I find it works best with 3 layers of each).

Beat the eggs with salt and pepper to taste and pour evenly over the layers in the dish. Cover with plastic wrap and refrigerate overnight.

Preheat the oven to 350°. Drizzle top of the dish with cream and bake for 45 minutes to 1 hour until puffy and slightly brown. Serve immediately.
Serves 4 to 6.

Jane Seymour during filming of Dr. Quinn's wedding day in 1995.

Beth Sullivan, executive producer of Dr. Quinn, Medicine Woman and head writer.

The entire cast of Dr. Quinn, Medicine Woman—and not a bite to eat.

Happy Meals to You

Georgann Johnson is a warm-hearted and brilliant woman with a wicked sense of humor. She tells stories with a flair and is also a good listener who can talk you through a problem until you can see the solution. She is the mother of this clan of "Quinn sisters," though she is in actuality not more than a couple of years older than I.

She is a gourmet cook who entertains often, and one of her best-loved preparations is this soup. Thank you, Georgann, for letting us have this.

Georgann Johnson.

CARROT/GINGER SOUP

3 teaspoons butter
2¼ cups diced onions
6 cups sliced carrots
4½ tablespoons grated or chopped fresh
    ginger
6 cups chicken broth
¾ cup (or more) fresh squeezed orange
    juice
½ cup light cream
    Salt to taste
    Sour cream
    Chives, finely snipped

In a medium casserole that can be heated on the stovetop, cook the onions in the butter until soft, about 3 or 4 minutes. Do not brown. Add the sliced carrots, ginger, and chicken broth. Bring to a boil, reduce the heat to low, and simmer, covered, until the carrots are very tender (25 to 30 minutes or more). Cool a few minutes. Blend (in batches) in the blender and return to the casserole or a bowl. Add the orange juice, light cream, and salt. Refrigerate, if not serving within about 2 hours. Reheat to serve and top with a dollop of sour cream and a sprinkle of chives. Taste and add more orange juice, chicken broth, and/or cream to thin if necessary.

Note: This may sound like a lot of ginger but it needs to be "zippy."
Serves 6 to 8.

The Quinn gang's all here! Arriving from Boston (again), I come down the back of the train, while Mother (Georgann Johnson) is in the center of the crowd.

The Perfect Blend

Frank Collison, who played Horace Bing on *Dr. Quinn,* has a lovely family, a wife and two daughters who often visited the set. He is as kind and gentle a person as the one he portrayed on the show, and it was a pleasure to work with him.

He sent this wonderful smoothie recipe saying, "I used to know how to cook but after nine years of marriage to the world's greatest improvisational cook, my skills have atrophied. My wife Sheila can make a five-course meal out of a handful of pasta, some mushrooms, and a tomato. About the only thing I still make are smoothies, hence this recipe. Smoothies are what I make when I have one of those 5:18 A.M. set calls. In order not to wake up the rest of the family, I stash the blender inside a cabinet before I turn it on. This is very important."

Thank you, Frank, and bless you.

Frank Collison, Horace Bing on Dr. Quinn, Medicine Woman.

FRANK'S EARLY MORNING SMOOTHIE

This recipe is designed for the half-awake or hung-over early riser. It requires no measuring and is virtually foolproof. I should know. I was inspired to make smoothies by the cooks out on the set of Dr. Quinn, Medicine Woman. *They would greet me at 5:30 in the morning with a fresh smoothie. Since I'm not a coffee drinker, their fantastic smoothies were my wake-up call.*

Ingredients:
  A big glass of orange juice
  A handful of frozen strawberries
  A frozen banana (the one that got too ripe and you tossed in the freezer last week), remove the peel by zapping the frozen banana in the microwave for about 30 seconds
  A big glop of plain yogurt (I prefer the tangy Armenian brands, none of that sweetened stuff)

Extras: You may throw in some of whatever squishy fruit you have on hand. I like pulpy orange juice so I sometimes toss in a couple of slices of orange. I also like kiwi, blueberries, mangoes, and papayas. Subtle-tasting fruits like honeydew don't seem to work. Forget about pears or apples, the blender can't handle them.

Put the yogurt in the blender first, and then add the orange juice. This is very important; if you slop the yogurt in after, you are likely to splatter juice all over your bathrobe (or whatever you wore to bed). If you or others are still asleep, place the blender in the closet or stash it in a cabinet before you start blending. No one likes being awakened by a snarling Mixmaster. Now make sure you have the lid on the blender. No one likes cleaning the ceiling. Hit the highest speed button and slowly add the frozen banana (did you peel it?) and frozen strawberries.

By using frozen fruit you avoid having to use ice cubes which are very noisy in a blender and add nothing to the taste. Overripe bananas are best because they have the most flavor and no one will eat them any other way. While the blender is blending, you can go find your glasses and hunt around for any extras you feel like adding. If you add enough fruit, you should get a really nice thick smoothie, which is, as all smoothie drinkers know, the best kind. Drink slowly to avoid brain freeze. Be sure to make extra because everyone who is awakened by the blender will ask for some of yours.

Heart of the West

Because of the stress and strain of putting out a one-hour weekly TV series with a large cast, animals, and children, there is no time for prima donnas, male or female. They must all work together, and I think anyone on *Dr. Quinn* would agree that Barbara Babcock, who played Dorothy Jennings so well, is the epitome of a team player.

Having had a long career on stage and screen, she also writes. And lest I make her sound dour and plodding, she is anything but. Always ready with a smile or a laugh, always eager to help or offer advice, she is a true life force, one that everyone is drawn to.

Here is her wonderful recipe she sent for you.

"This is a recipe from a cookbook written by General Patton's daughter, called *The Rolling Kitchen* (referring to the cavalry kitchens out West and on up until World War I). So in the spirit of Dr. Quinn and my own heritage of four generations in the cavalry (from my father back to my great-great-grandfather), here is a favorite."—Barbara Babcock

Barbara Babcock.

MEXICAN CHICKEN WITH ORANGE JUICE

The advantage of this dish is you can cook it in advance (even a day ahead), then remove the chicken and condiments, add the flour, thicken, and reheat everything on low. It actually tastes better the next day.

1	cut-up fryer
3	tablespoons butter
12	blanched almonds
1	cup chopped pineapple
2	cups orange juice
	Salt or pepper
½	cup seeded raisins
	Dash ground cloves or cinnamon
1	tablespoon all-purpose flour mixed to a paste with 2 tablespoons cold water

In an electric frying pan brown the chicken, then add all of the other ingredients except the flour paste. Cover the skillet and simmer for 45 minutes. Add the flour paste and cook until the gravy thickens, about 8 minutes. Garnish with avocado slices. Serve sauce separately.
Serves 3 or 4.

Pony Express

I've never had a problem with weight, save a pound or two fluctuation now and then, so imagine my surprise in 1997 when, stepping on a scale at a doctor's office, I found I was at least seven pounds over my fighting weight. And I was to do another *Dr. Quinn* in about six weeks.

Cheri Ingle, costume designer on the show, had not only had some gorgeous clothes made for my "Rebecca" the year before, but had had my very own corset sewn to my dimensions.

What to do? I, like most people, hate to diet. I'd never learned how because I didn't need to. So, I cut out fat and yes, the pounds melted away, and, by the time of the fittings for the new episodes, I got back to the weight I'd been before,.

This is a salad dressing I devised that garnered compliments. After our guests enjoyed it, I told them it was totally fat free, and they were amazed.

Getting some exercise before filming—the horse that is.

ELLIE'S ORIENTAL SALAD

I'll give you the ingredients, the amounts are up to you.

Boston lettuce, washed, dried, and torn into big pieces
Scallions, washed, dried, and sliced
Canned sliced water chestnuts, drained
Canned mandarin oranges, drained
Canned Chinese noodles (optional; these have some fat)

In a salad bowl combine the lettuce, scallions, water chestnuts, mandarin oranges, and Chinese noodles.

Dressing:
¼ cup good honey
¼ cup Dijon mustard
1 tablespoon wine vinegar
¼ teaspoon ground ginger
Poppy seeds, optional

Mix all together and dress the salad lightly.

In one of Rebecca's period garments.

Ready for a funeral in a 1997 episode of Dr. Quinn.

Direct Hit

Alicia Lewis was a Directors Guild of America trainee, who joined the production staff of *Dr. Quinn.* She loves to bake and she brought this cake to the set to share one day during the '97 season. It is phenomenal!

It is a family recipe and she has made her own mark on it with the "variation." Do take note.

COMPANY SPICE CAKE

2 cups sugar
3 eggs, well beaten
1½ cups oil
3 cups all-purpose flour
1 teaspoon salt
1 teaspoon ground cinnamon
1 teaspoon baking soda
½ teaspoon cloves
1 teaspoon ground nutmeg
3 cups finely chopped apples
1 cup chopped pecans

Icing:
1 teaspoon vanilla extract
1 cup confectioners' sugar
¼ to ⅓ cup milk

In a large bowl combine the sugar, eggs, and oil, and mix well. In a separate bowl sift the dry ingredients together and add to the sugar mixture. Fold in the apples and pecans. Pour into a well-greased and floured bundt pan. Bake at 350° for 1 hour.

For icing, mix the ingredients together to a good consistency. Glaze the cooled cake with the icing.

Variation (Alicia's cake): Omit the cloves and nutmeg. Add cinnamon. Reduce the oil to 1 cup and the flour to 2 cups. Add 2 teaspoons of vanilla extract. Bake in a 9 x 13 x 2-inch greased cake pan. For icing, blend ½ cup of margarine, 1 cup brown sugar, and ¼ cup evaporated milk. Boil for 2½ minutes and pour over the hot cake. *Serves 10 to 12.*

Memories of Mother

My mother. She hated to have her picture taken when she was younger, but got to liking it when she was older. She was a pistol. We didn't always get along, but we always understood that those moments were temporary.

She was a "saver." Boy, was she ever! And so without that trait, this book could never have been done.

In 1994 on my way to New York to help James and Martha after the birth of their second child, Lily, Mother smilingly said to me, "Well, I guess you're taking over now"—meaning that she had always been the one to run to the aid of one of us after the birth of a baby.

Three days later she fell asleep with her glasses on, one of her beloved mystery books open on her lap, and a chocolate chip cookie half-eaten on a napkin beside her. She was ninety-seven years old.

She went to be with the Lord, and not a day goes by that I don't miss her. Thank you, Mother, for everything.

Her grandson, my boy Chris, insists that we include this recipe.

NANA'S MEAT LOAF

2	pounds ground round steak
1	pound ground pork shoulder
2	slices white bread, moistened in milk or water, liquid squeezed out and crumbled
1	small onion, finely chopped
2	tablespoons finely snipped fresh parsley
2	eggs
2	to 3 tablespoons ketchup or Heinz 57 sauce
½	teaspoon dried basil, crushed
	Salt and pepper to taste

Mother and me in 1939.

In a large bowl combine the ground meat, bread, onion, parsley, and eggs. Squish it all together until well blended. Shape into a loaf and place it in a baking pan. Make an indentation with the side of your hand in the loaf—either criss-cross or diagonal—and put in the ketchup or 57 sauce. Bake at 350° for 1 hour and 30 minutes or until there is no pink in the juices.

Do not put this in a loaf pan. You want it brown on all sides and free-standing.
Serves 6 to 8.

Brian with his Nana in 1959.

My Mother at her 95th birthday party.

This is my favorite picture of Mother, splashing her feet in Peggy Ramey's pool.

That's A Wrap

I hope that you've had as much fun reading this collection as I have had putting it together. One of the best parts is having some of my recipes in one place. Now I can find them when I need them—instead of shuffling through scraps of paper and frantically looking for just the right one.

The very best part was contacting old friends and co-workers, who were so generous with their favorites. I'm still a recipe collector and life goes on, so who knows? I may be meeting you between the covers of a book again some day. Until then, enjoy!

Index